DR. BROTH AND OLLIE'S
BRAIN-BOGGLING
SEARCH FOR THE LOST LUGGAGE

*Across Time and Space
in Eighty Puzzles*

MICHAEL ABRAMS & JEFFREY WINTERS

Illustrations by Marc Rosenthal

A FIRESIDE BOOK
Published by Simon & Schuster
New York London Toronto Sydney Singapore

FIRESIDE

Rockefeller Center

1230 Avenue of the Americas

New York, NY 10020

Text copyright © 2000 by Michael Abrams and Jeffrey Winters

Illustrations copyright © 2000 by Marc Rosenthal

Designed by Bonni Leon-Berman

Puzzle and solution art by Outhouse Studio

Manufactured in the United States of America

10   9   8   7   6   5   4   3   2   1

Library of Congress Cataloging-in-Publication Data

Abrams, Michael.

    Dr. Broth and Ollie's brain-boggling search for the lost luggage : across time and space in eighty puzzles / Michael Abrams & Jeffrey Winters ; illustrations by Marc Rosenthal.

      p.   cm.

    1. Mathematical recreations.   I. Title: Doctor Broth and Ollie's brain-boggling search for the lost luggage.   II. Winters, Jeffrey.   III. Title.

QA95 .A27 2000

793.7'4—dc21   00-058695

ISBN 0-684-87001-0

MANY THANKS TO OUR EDITOR STEPHEN MORROW
AND TO CRAIG KASPER, DARREN RIGBY,
BILL MICHAELS, CAROLYN STANLEY, BRIDGET COPLEY,
AS WELL AS THE NATIONAL PUZZLERS LEAGUE.

CONTENTS

Dr. Broth Meets Ollie and McGuffin

A MELANCHOLIC DR. BROTH, professor emeritus of non-Euclidean paleolinguistic astrohistoriography, strolled about the topiary gardens in the campus arboretum. Amid the transected cones of spruce and tetrahedral hedges, he sought solace.

He had just returned from a conference on the Hyde-body problem, and his luggage—one bulging attaché case—had not appeared on the airport's baggage claim. And what was it that strained the seams of the missing luggage? The professor's only copy of his just-finished manuscript on indopithecine tribal kinship equations. His life's work.

As pleasing as the geometric horticulture was, it didn't seem to be helping his mood. He had luggage on the brain. Lost in thought, he turned a corner on the gravel path and came face to face with a leaf-covered ruminant.

Ollie, the friendly gardener, was trimming its tail with hedge clippers.

"Why, it's a llama!" Dr. Broth gleefully exclaimed.

"Pthppppt," the beast answered, spitting at the doctor.

"He's an alpaca—and very sensitive on the issue," said Ollie.

Dr. Broth was taken aback.

"Surely that's because throughout the Andes alpaca wool is considered much finer than that of the llama. When I was doing field research on the textile trade in Ecuador—"

"Oh, no, sir. McGuffin is just proud of the fact that only alpacas can travel through space and time," said Ollie.

"You mean he can exploit multidimensional rifts in the space-time continuum?"

"I don't know how he does it, but he can take you anywhere you want to go."

"But I can't guarantee *when* you'll get there," said the alpaca under his breath.

The professor was already considering the possibilities.

"Do you think you could take me to my briefcase? According to my airline timetable, the airplane with my briefcase is supposedly on its way to Chicago."

"Sure," said Ollie, "just climb aboard."

Achocolate Now!

IN AN INSTANT, DR. BROTH and Ollie, on the back of McGuffin the alpaca, arrived at what used to be O'Hare International Airport. But much to the doctor's dismay, there was no airport in sight, only the ruins of civilization.

"Where are we?" asked Dr. Broth.

"It's not a matter of where, but when," said Ollie. "McGuffin doesn't always arrive on time. In this case, I think we're about a hundred years too late."

The trio scouted about the desolate landscape for a bit. Behind a heap of broken bricks, they spotted a shabby urchin.

"Have you seen the baggage-claim?" asked Dr. Broth.

The urchin stared back suspiciously.

"This child seems to be suffering from some form of malnutrition," said the doctor.

"Maybe we should give him some food," said Ollie.

"What he really needs is a flea collar," said McGuffin, looking down his snout.

The child's lips twisted in an attempt to speak.

"Ch-Ch-Chocolate. Need chocolate."

"I think we'd all like a piece of chocolate," said Dr. Broth cheerily as he brought out a chunk of an old Tuberone bar—probably the last on the planet.

The four of them stared at the little triangle in the doctor's hand.

"I don't see how we're going to split it up into equal bits," said Dr. Broth. Better just give half to me and half to the llam—I mean McGuffin here—so he'll have some energy to get home."

"I think we can split it into four equal sections," said Ollie.

"But what about the peanuts? We'll have to divide up the peanuts in the chocolate as well. Protein deficiency is one of the first stages of starvation. The people of nonequatorial Guinea get most of their protein from—"

Ollie the gardener interrupted. "I think I can evenly divide the chocolate so that everyone gets two peanuts."

Ollie, Dr. Broth, and McGuffin devoured their chocolate sections. The urchin, however, carefully wrapped his piece in the remaining gold foil and tucked it away.

"Well, what do you know," said Dr. Broth, "here's another piece in my right pocket. This one seems to be from an almond bar. But it doesn't look like we'll be able to divide it the same way, Ollie."

Ollie briefly inspected the second piece.

"Actually, this one can also be divided into four equal sections so that each piece has the same number of almonds. But they won't all be the same shape as our first bits."

Die Betting

THE URCHIN ATE THE second helping and motioned the others to follow him.

"Why didn't he eat the first one?" asked McGuffin.

"Maybe he's allergic to peanuts," suggested Ollie.

They climbed rubble heap after rubble heap. Each heap they climbed revealed a larger one ahead, and the farther they went, the more rubble heaps appeared. Soon all the rubble heaps seemed to merge into one gigantic Matterhorn of rubble. They climbed to a plateau swarming with children. Many of the urchins had claimed a small area as their own. Spread out before them were bicycle parts, jewelry, rubber bands, various grubby fruits, and other invaluable objects they'd found. Goods were being exchanged in every direction. A ragged girl of eight or nine traded a comic book for a can of machine oil. The ragged boy who received the comic book turned to another ragged customer and swapped a small crossbow for a box of bubble gum.

The urchin led his new friends to a corner where shouting children were surrounded by a small crowd. He edged his way in, and the others followed as best they could.

Inside the throng, a circle was drawn on the ground where the children were betting their belongings. A grinning, big-nosed kid was filling a sack with what he'd just won. When he'd finally cleared the circle of the last of his booty—a whistle and an Etch-A-Sketch key ring—the urchin guide stepped forward.

An Urchin Leads the Way

A hush fell over the children as he slowly pulled his remaining chocolate from his pocket. He unfolded the wrapper one corner at a time. Then he placed the chocolate, on top of the wrapper, in the circle. The children gasped. A girl quickly stepped forward. She placed a gold-plated knife, a working watch, and two bottles of ketchup in the ring. A frail boy with blond curls followed suit, pulling a meat grinder and a solar-powered calculator from his bag and laying them down before the crowd. Then a fat boy dragged in a moped, carefully keeping it away from the chocolate. No one else had anything of enough value to bet against the morsel of Tuberone.

Six dice marked with strange symbols lay on the ground. The girl picked them up and gave them a toss. She quickly grouped the results into three pairs. The crowd began to chatter. A tall boy in a tattered tuxedo stepped into the circle and called out, "One!" The girl stepped back, hopeful but still anxious. Then the boy with the moped threw the dice. After he'd grouped his results, a sigh of awe and a few claps came from the spectators. The boy in the tuxedo announced the result: "Two!" The frail boy stepped to the edge of the circle and threw. The crowd murmured as he grouped the dice and received a score of one. Next the urchin

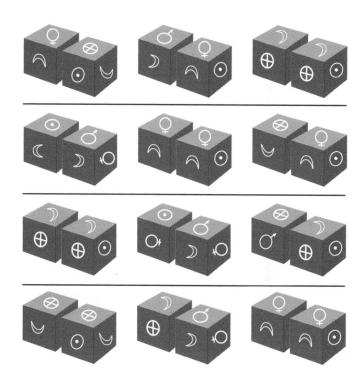

took the dice and rolled them. His pairs elicited a moan of sympathy mixed with chuckles of derision. "I don't think that was the best possible grouping," Ollie whispered to McGuffin. The boy in the tuxedo sneered as he called out, "Zero!" The urchin stepped back unhappily as the boy who'd put in the moped reached for the chocolate.

"Hold on! Just one moment!" said Dr. Broth, stepping forward. "The game's not over yet, is it?"

The children shook their heads.

"Then I'm next." Dr. Broth lifted up McGuffin and put him in the circle, nearly crushing the chocolate.

The doctor picked up the dice, shook them a few times, blew into his hands, and said, "Snake eyes, snake eyes." Then he looked at the symbols on the dice, "Er, no, never mind that." With a great softball swing he threw the dice forward.

They rolled to a halt in the dust.

Dr. Broth stared blankly at the results.

"Eh, Ollie. Do you think you could help me put these together? The symbols are a little small with my bad eyesight, you know."

"Oh, yes," said Ollie as he broke free from the crowd. "I'll be glad to put them in what's most likely to be the best grouping possible."

Riff Tiff

OLLIE AND DR. BROTH'S deft maneuvering won the chocolate, which the urchin devoured in front of the drooling crowd. Then he filled a sack with the ketchup, pocketed the knife, mounted the moped, and gave McGuffin a tug. All the children looked longingly at the alpaca.

"You can't have him," said Dr. Broth to the envious crowd.

They left the market area and followed the urchin to a cave dug into a great mound of rubble. "Tonight: Mutanzo Brass Band, All-Age Show" was written in white chalk on the black rock outside the entrance. The urchin tapped on his new watch and beckoned them inside.

The cave was packed with ragged children. Hundreds of them milled about, eagerly awaiting the appearance of the Mutanzo Brass Band. When they'd waited so long that Dr. Broth's knees and feet were aching, five children climbed onto the makeshift stage at the back of the cave. Cheers and whistles filled the cavern.

A trumpeter with a beaten up trumpet, a tuba player with a rusty tuba, a trombonist with a dented trombone, a French-horn player with a scratched-up French horn, and a tiny boy with a huge bass drum tried to find their places on the small stage. The trumpeter moved up front, but the French-horn player felt that that was where he should stand. The boy with the bass drum started arguing with the tuba player over who should stand in the back. The band members swapped places, bickered, and elbowed one another for a good five minutes.

When they'd finally decided on an arrangement, they still couldn't get settled. The tuba player was taking up too much space, claimed the trombonist. The trombone's slide was going to hit him in the leg, whined the trumpet player. The bass drum was inching into his territory, said the French-horn player. Finally they decided to divide up the stage into five equal sections with some masking tape. No one would be allowed out of his allotted space.

The stage was a mere ten feet by ten feet, and all they had was twenty-six feet of masking tape. As they tried to divide up the stage, another shouting match broke out among the musicians.

"Is this a concert or a circus?" asked McGuffin. "Ollie, can you straighten these clowns out?"

"Ah, I think so," said Ollie. He then carefully divided the stage into five sections of equal area using less than the available twenty-six feet of masking tape.

Rest in Peace

ONCE THE MUSICIANS STUCK the masking tape to the stage, found their places, and tested out their elbow room, they launched into a spirited version of Scarlatti's "Venere e Adone." The crowd went wild. An exhilarating version of The Dirty Dozen Brass Band's "Mr. Flintstone Meets the President" followed. McGuffin and Ollie bobbed along to the rhythm.

"A vigorous approach to the old chestnut," said Dr. Broth. "Intelligent yet unpretentious, clever and catchy, but not insidious. An ironic usage of cliché in genre-merging."

Ollie shrugged his shoulders in sync with the bass drum.

The third tune started with only drum and tuba. A heavy backbeat established, the French-horn player began his solo. As the performance built, some children in the audience began stealing looks at McGuffin. But if they saw Ollie watching them, the children quickly looked away. The French-horn player's solo grew louder and louder while more and more children stared over their shoulders at McGuffin. Soon their stares were pressing in on him from all sides.

"There's more than a few quotes thrown into this artist's playing," said Dr. Broth, oblivious to the changing atmosphere and constant glances. "He's blowing through the history of music, giving it a twist at every turn, and offering a wry commentary on the arbitrary success of the few who have risen to the top of the ensemble industry."

Ollie could not accept this critique: "I hate to disagree with you, doctor, but the message is more along the lines of 'Let's steal that alpaca and eat him for dinner.' I know you're enjoying the music, but I think we ought to get out of here."

"I don't see how you get that message from the music," said Dr. Broth.

"It's the notes they're playing," said Ollie, dragging McGuffin and Dr. Broth toward the exit. "That French-horn player spells out what he wants to say very clearly on his instrument, if you listen carefully."

Singeing in the Rain

THE SYMPATHETIC URCHIN AND a friend of his, who also understood the danger of the musical message, helped Ollie drag the reluctant Dr. Broth and oblivious McGuffin out of the cave club, pulling them as fast as they could over the lumpy terrain. A few children at the club's entrance noticed the escape and whistled up a posse to chase the strangers.

Sensing the determination of their pursuers, Dr. Broth, Ollie, McGuffin and their two diminutive guides ran faster than they thought possible. Exhausted, they ducked into a hole in the side of one of the mounds. McGuffin and Dr. Broth tried to pause so that their eyes could adjust to the darkness, but Ollie tugged them forward. They were in a tunnel. Complete darkness surrounded them after a few feet.

"I was enjoying the oompah music back there," complained McGuffin. "Where are you dragging me?"

"I thought we were saving your life," whispered Ollie, "though I have to admit, I don't know where we're going. These two kids are probably as hungry as the rest of them in that club. Maybe they're trying to capture you just for themselves. Stay on your guard."

Only McGuffin, a natural on rough terrain, managed to avoid scuffing his knees as they scrambled through the tunnel in darkness. The doctor lagged behind the others. Eventually a spot of gray light appeared, and they arrived at an opening that looked out onto more barren landscape. In another mound a few feet from where they stood, they saw another hole waiting for them. But it was raining.

Ollie and Dr. Broth stared at the ground in shock. Where rain landed, small puffs of smoke appeared. At first they thought it was dust from the force of the heavy droplets, but the puffs kept on appearing after the ground and all the rubbish on it was wet.

"Acid rain," said Ollie.

"Must be some kind of fallout," said Dr. Broth.

"We can't go out in that," said McGuffin.

The urchins, however, were unfolding raincoats they'd kept under their shirts. They handed them to Ollie and Dr. Broth, suggesting, it seemed, that they cross to the other mound together. Then one of them could return with the two ponchos. They could repeat the process so that all five of them could cross protected from the rain.

Protection from the Elements

"It's a good idea," said Ollie to Dr. Broth, "but I don't think that any one of us should have to stay at any time with the two of them. Their intentions seem good, but we don't know them too well. And they're very hungry."

The sound of their pursuers echoed from deep within the tunnel. Though Dr. Broth still wasn't sure precisely why they were fleeing, the sound of the approaching famished urchins scared him.

"We'd better hurry," he said, "we need to think of the quickest way to get us across. McGuffin seems to be the fastest of the three of us on this terrain. I'm probably the slowest."

"If we do it so none of us have to ever be alone with the two of them, there's just one way to get us across as fast as possible, assuming McGuffin will need two raincoats," said Ollie thoughtfully.

Laze before You Leap

AFTER ESCAPING THE HUNGRY mob, the group made their way to the urchins' dwelling place. There they enjoyed a soak in the urchins' spring-fed Jacuzzi.

"Why is it," Dr. Broth asked McGuffin, "that during that horrendous chase scene you didn't just jump us to some new time or place?"

"We alpacas have to feel comfortable and relaxed before we can make the leap. Like now, for instance," said McGuffin, submerging himself in bubbles.

"The temperature is optimal," said Dr. Broth. "In fact, I find that a bit puzzling. Chicago is in the midst of a vast sedimentary plain with very little hydrothermal potential. It seems unlikely to find a hot spring here."

"Perhaps the water's radiant glow is a clue," said Ollie.

No Lefties in Moscow

TOWELING OFF, DR. BROTH checked his airline timetable, and realized that back in the twenty-first century, the plane with his briefcase had gone ahead to Moscow. Duly relaxed, McGuffin hoofed it through the space-time continuum with Ollie and the doctor on his back, hoping to get to Russia before

Taxiski Rideski

the plane. At the baggage-claim counter, they discovered that they'd arrived too late. A helpful attendant suggested inquiring at the Office of Lost Luggage in downtown Moscow. The trio set out but were rudely

informed by a man in a drab-looking uniform that alpacas were not allowed in the streets without a license plate. So they hailed a cab. But when the cabbie heard where they were going, he shook his head.

"You can't get there from here," he said.

"Nonsense. I'll direct you," announced Dr. Broth as he unfolded a map of the city. Nearly every street was one-way. As they drove through the city, Broth barked out directions.

"Turn left here," he commanded.

"*Nyet*," replied the cabbie.

"Well, turn left at the next block."

"*Nyet*," said the cabbie.

"Can't you make any left turns?"

"*Nyet*," said the cabbie. "All left turns are prohibited."

He parked the taxi on the side of the street.

"Well then, my good man, how does one get to the Office of Lost Luggage?"

"You can't get there from here," said the cabbie.

"I'm not getting out of this cab," said McGuffin. "I don't feel like spending the night in a Russian prison for walking down the street."

Ollie glanced at the map. "I think I see a way to get us there without breaking any traffic laws."

Bathroom Bureaucracy

"LUGGAGE? WE HAVE NO luggage," said the official behind the desk.

"It says Office of Lost Luggage on the door," said Dr. Broth, thumbing through a Russian dictionary, "though it's a little hard to read."

"That is because this used to be the office of the KGB; before that, it was the office of the MOOP; before that, the office of the NVD; before that, the office of the NKVD; and before that, the office of the GPU."

"Delightful anacronyms, my good man," said Dr. Broth, "but is this or is this not the Office of Lost Luggage?"

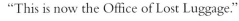

"This is now the Office of Lost Luggage."

"And you have no lost luggage?"

"We have no luggage."

"You don't have a heavy brown attaché case," asked Dr. Broth, "a little worn, perhaps very worn, leather handle, dull brass clasps? A frayed border on either side, slightly darker than the rest, no side pockets, about half a foot wide—"

"We have no luggage."

"Baggage? A bag. A briefbag, heavy, brown, leather handle—"

"We have no luggage."

"Excuse me, sir," interjected Ollie. "If a piece of luggage happens to be misplaced, what normally would be the procedure for dealing with it?"

"If a piece of luggage is misplaced, it is searched for foreign currency, blue jeans, and toilet paper. It is then sent back to the destination from which it came."

"Vere the luggage is searched for foreign currency, counterfeit blue jeans, and toilet paper and sent to the destination vrom vich it came," said the alpaca.

"Correct."

"You wouldn't happen to know if there was any misplaced luggage on a plane from O'Hare?" asked Ollie.

The functionary typed away on his TRS-80.

"Yes. That luggage has been sent back to O'Hare. . . . No, I'm sorry, it seems that it is currently on a cargo flight to Glasgow. My apologies."

"Off we go, I suppose," said McGuffin.

"Well, yes. But first I'd like to visit the rest room," said the doctor. "Could you tell me where I can find such a thing?"

"Yes, this I can do, comrade. But I'm afraid it's a long story. When this was the office of the GPU, the bath-

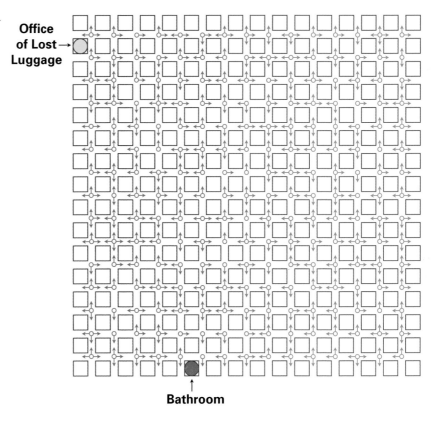

room was right next door, but when the NKVD took over the building, they turned it into a storage room and moved the bathroom down the hall. When the NVD moved in, they changed the new bath-room into a coatroom. When the MOOP moved in, they stationed an intern at the coatroom and moved the bathroom upstairs. When the KGB wanted a sauna, they added tiles and steam and moved the bathroom into the room we are in. Then they wanted to put the Office of Lost Luggage in the lowest place imaginable, so they put me here, and we had to move the bathroom yet again. The building has been through so many changes that it's quite pointless for me to give you directions." He handed a sheet of paper to Dr. Broth. "This is a map of the floor we're on," he said. "In order to avoid the hall monitors, you must go only in the direction the arrows point."

But when he stepped outside of the Office of Lost Luggage, the doctor didn't know what to do.

"I'll never find my way there. And the situation is, er, urgent."

"Don't worry," said Ollie. "I'll draw the shortest path from where we are now to the bathroom."

A Blueprint for Disaster

DR. BROTH TROTTED DOWN the hall with a finger on the path Ollie had traced out. The others watched him until he disappeared around a corner.

"I hope he makes it back," said the official.

"Maybe we should have gone with him," said Ollie.

"What I don't understand," said McGuffin as they sat down in the office, "is why you don't just build a new building instead of changing this one so many times and shoving people and whole departments into closets and bathrooms."

"Interesting, comrade," said the official. "We once had a new building planned for all these burgeoning departments. It was going to be a beautiful example of the Soviet aesthetic: a smooth, gray cement exterior, square windows, false ceilings, fluorescent lights. And with the prosperity of the great Soviet socialist republics behind it, there were bathrooms for every floor." The official leaned back in his chair and raised his eyes to the ceiling proudly and a little dreamily.

"Well, what happened?" asked McGuffin.

"Sadly, the logistics of the revolution delayed the project. The Bureau of Architecture needed a place to work so the government put them in this building. Then, when their plans were approved, the Bureau

A Run for the Bathroom

of Construction needed a place to set up shop, so the government kicked out the architects. Somewhere along the way, blueprints for the new building got mixed up with blueprints for a school—they're remarkably similar—and now nobody can tell what's what."

"Could we have a look at them?" asked Ollie. "Just to pass the time till Dr. Broth comes back," he added in response to a suspicious look.

The official opened a big filing cabinet and rooted around for a while. Then he rooted around some more. Then he swore. After about ten minutes of rooting and swearing, he came up with six large blueprints. He spread them out on the table before Ollie. Three of the prints depicted the side of a building, and three others showed some floor plans.

"Not all of these are of the same building," said the functionary. "Some may be of the school, and some may be of the new building."

Ollie looked at the prints and rubbed his chin.

"It may not be enough to start construction right away, but I can tell that five of these prints belong to one building and one belongs to another."

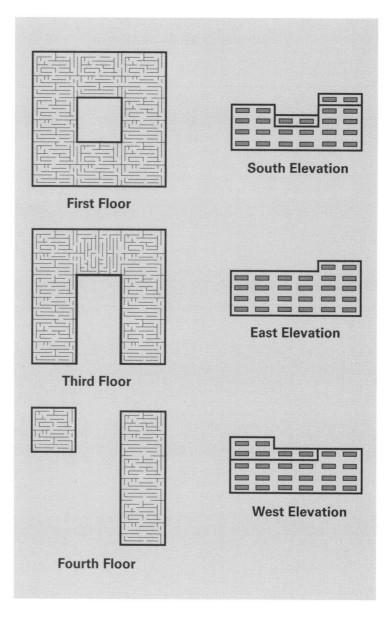

First Floor

Third Floor

Fourth Floor

South Elevation

East Elevation

West Elevation

Number One or Number Two?

"WHAT'S TAKING DR. BROTH so long?" asked McGuffin.

"Maybe he's lost, despite our precautions," suggested the official.

"I'll go check," said Ollie.

"But he's got the map."

"Don't worry, I've got that all in my head."

Ollie left McGuffin and the functionary to talk about the price of mohair hats and vodka. He zipped down a few hallways, around a few corners, and soon happened upon Dr. Broth. Agitated and red faced, Dr. Broth paced back and forth in front of the bathroom door. On the door was a strange lock made of six concentric circles, each with six prime numbers on it.

"What's the problem?" asked Ollie.

"I think there's someone inside."

"Did you knock?" asked Ollie.

"No. But the door is locked. I didn't want to disturb whoever's in there."

Ollie gave the door a few raps. No one responded.

"The official probably just forgot to give you the combination. You stay here—it's not a good idea to move around in the condition you're in. I'll be right back."

Ollie hurried back to the lost-luggage office. The alpaca and the Russian seemed to be getting along very well. Interrupting a tirade from McGuffin on

Russian economic reform, Ollie asked for the combination to the bathroom.

"Brezhnev's eyebrows! Comrade, I'm very sorry. I forgot to tell you. The KGB installed that lock in a fit of paranoia. I guess they were afraid spies would smuggle top-secret information out through the toilet. Just line up the circles so each row of numbers adds up to a prime number. Three of those sums will be the same number."

Leaving them to their vodka and pickled beets, which they were consuming liberally, Ollie made his way back as fast as he could. He found Dr. Broth squatting on the floor, bouncing up and down.

"It won't be long now," he said.

Ollie spun the circles a few times and opened the door.

Stranded

WITH DR. BROTH RELIEVED, they entered the great continuum once again, headed for Glasgow. But a warp in spacetime threw them off and something green and peculiar happened before they landed. Instead of appearing at the airport as planned, Ollie and McGuffin found themselves in the lab of the great geneticist Igor Wilma.

And Dr. Broth was nowhere to be seen.

"What happened to the doctor?" Ollie asked.

"I think he may have been vaporized," whispered McGuffin. "We passed pretty close to that green wormhole."

"Oh my!" cried Ollie.

"I was getting sick of carrying that extra baggage anyhow," said the irritable alpaca.

Ollie didn't hear him. A dull glint on the alpaca had caught his eye. A row of something like fish scales stuck to the wool on either side of McGuffin. Slowly understanding what the scales were, he could barely hold back his tears.

"Ye seem a wee distraught," the geneticist said to Ollie through a slight overbite. "There anything I can do tae help?"

"We've—*sob*—lost our friend. There's nothing left of him but his toenails."

"Dinna fash yerself, laddie! Those minky things will do the trick. I can rebuild yer friend frae his DNA. If ye got two hundred thousand pounds, that is, o' course."

"I'm afraid we don't have any money. If we could find Dr. Broth's manuscript, maybe that would be worth something."

"Dr. Broth? Do ye say Dr. Broth? Ye don't mean *the* Dr. Broth?"

"I do, I do."

"Queen Mary's knickers! That non-Euclidean paleolinguistic astrohistoriographist owes me money. In 1969 he wagered twenty pounds that I'd not live tae see the day when a human being was cloned. Let's see . . . wi' interest . . . compounded hourly . . . late fee . . . that's nigh two million pounds he owes me.

We'll prove him wrong richt nou! Grab those toenails; maybe ye can help me with a few DNA strands."

"What could I do?" asked Ollie.

"Ye could put together the DNA sequence fur the outer rim o' his left nostril. Tae speed up the sequencing process, we usually chop up two or three long strands inta wee bits an' then stick 'em together in the correct order. Only problem is that there's always a fair bit o' o'erlap. The DNA sequence for the nostril is fifteen molecules long, each base represented by a letter. We hae seven overlapping fragments. Can ye put them together in the richt order?"

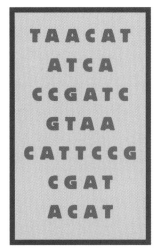

TAACAT
ATCA
CCGATC
GTAA
CATTCCG
CGAT
ACAT

Broth in Formation

Humorous DNA

"NEXT," CONTINUED THE GENETICIST, "we hae some strands fur his humerus."

"I didn't know there was anything humorous about him," said McGuffin.

"It's thirty molecules long and we hae nine fragments. Can ye put it together?" Wilma asked Ollie.

GTTC

TCAGC

TTCAAG

AAGAA

TACTG

AGCATTCAA

TCTTC

TACGTA

AAGTACG

Human or Alpaca?

"WHILE WE'RE WAITING FUR the good doctor tae incubate," said Wilma to the alpaca, "allow me tae pose a wee simple question. Seems we've got two types o' toenails here. One o' them doona seem quite like the others. Ye wouldn't happen tae ken who it belongs tae, would ye?"

"Er, I was taking care of some personal hygiene on the trip here," said McGuffin.

"Hmmmmm. Ye think ye can figure out who these strands belong tae? The sequence tae the right is alpaca DNA, the sequence tae the left, Dr. Broth's."

ALPACA DNA:

GCAGCAATCAATCCGTGACATATATCGCATAAGCGC

DR. BROTH'S DNA:

GCAGCAATCAATGCGTGACATATATAGCATAAGCGC

THE STRANDS:

GTGA	GCAGCAA
CGTGA	GCAATC
AGCA	ATATAGC
CAATG	TGCGTGACAT
AAGCGC	AATCA
CATATATA	TAGCATAA
	ATAAGC

Clonesomes

"I CAN'T WAIT TO SEE the cloning process in action," said Ollie as they sat down in front of an aquarium of bluish liquid to watch the new Dr. Broth grow.

"It's amazing," said McGuffin pointing to the fetus, "that all that could come from a toe-nail. And soon it will be Dr. Broth again."

"The miracle of life . . . ," said Ollie.

Hours later the fetus had only just become a baby. The sports coat had begun to emerge, but the patches hadn't yet developed.

"Soon . . . to . . . be . . . a . . . man," yawned McGuffin. "As-ton-ish-ing."

"We doona hae tae sit here," said Dr. Wilma, "I'll show ye another project o' mine."

He led them down a corridor to a steel door. Above the door handle was a black square. Wilma put his hand against it. An orange light flashed. Then Wilma bent down and pressed his face into the square. A green light came on and the door clicked open.

"Why did you have to put your face there?" asked Ollie.

"That black square scans my fingerprints an' reads the DNA in my cells. But, there's aye the possibility that some axe-wielding radge could get ahold o' my hand. But gettin' both my hands an' my hied is a wee bit harder." He pushed the door open and they stepped into an immaculate white room with thirty aquariums like the one that held Dr. Broth. But instead of fetuses, the aquariums held children, teenagers, and adults.

"Gang take a look," said Dr. Wilma, smiling.

Ollie and McGuffin approached the tanks.

"These children," said Ollie, "they look like you."

"And these teenagers," said McGuffin, "they look like you, too."

"Ay, my beastie. Yer eyes wark," said Wilma, now chuckling to himself. "They are me! In a sense."

"Is this going to be your own army?" asked Ollie.

"Or big band?" asked McGuffin.

"Are you trying to take over the world?" asked Ollie.

"Nae, just Scotland," said Wilma. "Ther're three political parties here," he continued, drawing them over to a table with a map of the region. "There's the Conservative Party an' the Labour Party, o' course. Bampots e'ry one of 'em. But then there's the Haggis Nationalist Party, the gretest party o' all, out tae re-

Tanks of Wilmas

store the glory o' Scotland, the gretest half an island on Earth."

Wilma pointed to the map on the table.

"This map shows the county we're in right nou. The *L*s are Labour residents; the *C*s, Conservatives; and the *H*s, Haggis Nationalists. They're going tae redivide the county inta four sections suin, an' I want tae be sure that ther'll be enough Haggis Nationalists in each section fur us tae tak' control. Un-

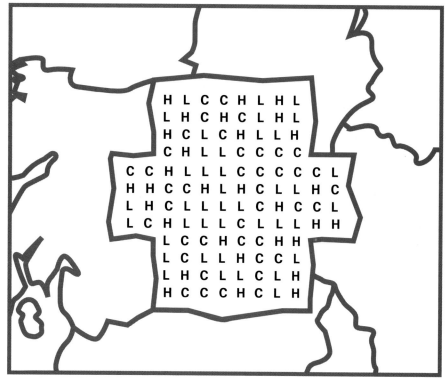

fortunately I hae tae find a way tae accelerate the development o' these clones so they're ready by the time the gerrymandering's done."

Ollie gave the map a once-over. "Hmmm. There already is a way that the county, as it is, can be divided into four sections of equal population so that the Haggis Nationalists can outnumber the Conservatives and Labourites in three of them."

"Of course, that would mean getting in good with the gerrymanderers," said McGuffin. "They don't happen to be Haggis Nationalists, do they?"

"Aye, they do."

"Great. Now you're free to use these folks here in your caber-tossing team."

Mama an' the Papas

A DEAFENING GONG SOUNDED, echoing among the tanks.

"Sounds like mair customers," said Wilma, "away wi' me, an' see the foolery I hae tae do tae fund my research."

They locked the door to the room of developing Wilmas and headed to the foyer. An agitated middle-aged woman, a ten-year-old girl, and four fuming men stood inside the door.

"Let's go home, mam. I doona want a faither."

"Havers, child, everyone wants a faither. 'Lo. Are ye Dr. Wilma?"

"The original," said the geneticist. "How can I help ye?"

"Weel, ah, these four men . . . ," she swept her hand to her side, "each seems tae think, fur some reason, that he's the faither o' Prissy 'ere. O' course, none o' them had any interest in the wean when she was just a baby, but nou that she's hied o' the debate team, leader o' the math club, silver-medal gymnast, Tai Kwon Do black belt, an' courted by Eton, she's got the eyes o' each o' 'em. Amazing, in' it?"

"Ach. That's no true, Val," said the biggest of the three men, a black-haired, bulbous-nosed brute in a red woolen cap, "Doona ye mind when I brought the wee bairn a stuffed sheep?"

"I said a stuffed animal would make a guid gift for the kimmer. I did nae mean some rotten cairciss frae a taxidermist's shop. Ye give the wein a fricht."

"That's richt," interjected the smallest of the men, a blond in a pinstripe suit. "Oniebodie can gie gifts. It's luv that a real faither shows. Haven't I visited ye e'ry day, Prissy?"

"Except fur Sundays," said the girl. "Ye're the mailman."

The mailman harrumphed.

"Wasn't I awa looking out fur Prissy's future?" said the third man, a wiry, bearded individual. "Trying tae teach her stuff so she could get on in life?"

PRISSY'S DNA

TTTCCCAATCCCCATGTCT
GTACTTGGTGGTACTAGAGT
AATGCTCGACATG
TCATGTCCGACGTCGACG
CGACGTTTACGGTT
TACTAGAGTTGTTACTTATACTAGAAATG
TGTCAATAATAATCATGTCC
CCATGTCTCCTCCTCCGCT

MOM'S DNA

TTACGGTTTCCCAAT
TTACGGAATGCTCGACATGTCA
ATGTCAATAATA
AATAATCATGTCCGACGTCG
ACGTTTACGGTTTCCCAATCCCT
CCAATCCCTTACGGTCCTCCTCCGCT
TGGTACTAGAGTTGTTACTTATTTA
GTACTTGGTGGTACTA

BULBOUS NOSE'S DNA

AGAAATAA
GTCCGACGTCGACGTTTACGGTTTCCCAATCCC
ATACTAGAAATGCT
AATAATCATGTCCGACGTCGA
TGGTGGTTTACGGGTTG
GTACTTGGTGG
CCTCCTCCG
TTTACGGGTTGTTACTTATACTAGA
AATGCTCGAACTAGA
AATAATAATCA
TGTCCGACGTCGACGTTTACGGTTTCC
CAATCCCATGTCTCCTCCTCCGCT

PINSTRIPE'S DNA

GTACTTGGTG
GTCATG
TCGTTGTTACTTATACTAGA
AATGCTCGACATGTCA
ATAATAA
TGGT
TCACGACGTCGACGTAC
TAGATTTCCCAATC
CCACTAGATCCTCCTCCGCT
CTTATACTAGAAATGCTCGA
TCGACATGTCAATAATAATGGTTCA
TGGTGGTCATGTCGTTGTTACTTATA
CGACGTACTAGATTTCCCA
TGGTTCACGAC

WIRY'S DNA

GTACTTGGTGGT
TTACGGGTTGTTACT
TATTTACGGA
ATGCTCGACATG
TCAATAATAATC
ATGTCCGACGTCGACGT
TTACGGT
TTCCCAATCCCCATGT
CTCCTCCTCCGCT
CGGGTTGTTACTTATTTACGGA
GTACTTGGTGGTT
ACGGTTTCCCAATCCCCATGTCTCCTCC
AATCATGTCCGA
GACATGTCAATAATA

NEVER HOME'S DNA

GTACTTGGTGGTGGTTC
AGTTGTTACTTATACTAG
AAATGCTCGAGGTTCAAA
TAATAATACTAGACGA
CGTCGACGTACTAGATTTCCCAATC
CCACTAGATCCTCCTCCGCT
TGGTGGTGGTTCAGTTGTTACTTATACT
TCAAATAATAATACTAGACGAC
AGATTTCCCAATCCCACTAGATC

"But I doona want tae be a pickpocket," said the girl.

"Nae a one o' ye understand faitherhood," said the mother. "A real faither doona show affection at all. Mine ne'er offered any encouragement o' any kaind and certainly wasn't e'er hame."

"Yeh, that's my argument," said the fourth man.

"Nou, nou," said Wilma, "we'll hae the matter resolved in two shakes o' a lamb's tail."

He led the gentlemen to a sterile room and took blood samples. Then, leaving the mother, daughter, and would-be fathers to stew, he took Ollie and McGuffin back to the lab. After running the samples through an Applied Biosystems machine, a Perkin-Elmer gadget, and a Thermo Instrument apparatus or two, Wilma called Ollie over.

"The way tae determine paternity is tae compare the DNA o' the mother an' child. Any place where it doona match up, then that DNA must hae come frae the faither. All ye hae tae do then is find the man who has all the richt genes. I think I've enough strands tae figure this'n out. Do ye think ye can do it?"

Ollie examined the list of strands for each of the parties in dispute. It wasn't long before he gave a little nod.

"I don't know how poor Val and Prissy are going to feel about it, but I do know who the father is."

"Given the choices, I think the lass 'ould be better off faitherless."

For Whom the Tolls Bill

"SINCE WE'VE HAD THE good luck to be here now—in the era to which I am accustomed—I think I'll call to see if that briefcase has arrived yet," said the newly formed Dr. Broth, still dripping from the tank's humerplasm.

He picked up the phone and dialed the number for the airport.

"Excuse me," he said, "has there been an update on the status of flight 1359?"

"One moment, please," came the woman's cool response, followed by the clack of computer keys. "Yes, that flight is right on time. In fact, it just entered Scottish airspace. It should begin a holding pattern over Glasgow in twenty minutes."

Dr. Broth hung up the phone.

"She says the cargo plane with my luggage will be over Glasgow soon."

"Let's hae a wee shuftey over to my friend Tycho Braveheart's observatory an' see if we can spot the plane coming in," said Wilma. "Mr. McGuffin, yer not at all Scottish, are ye now?" he asked conversationally.

"No," said McGuffin, "I'm from the South American highlands."

THE TIME-TRAVELING CREW piled into Wilma's car. Wilma sat in the driver's seat, scratching his head. Everyone was expecting him to rev the engine, step on the gas, and hurry to the observatory, but instead, he just sat there looking confused.

"If you're looking for your keys, they're in your hand," said McGuffin helpfully.

"Nae, nae, nae, it's not that," said Wilma, now putting the key into the ignition. "There's just sae monie ways tae get tae the observatory on our wily Scottish roads that I can ne'er decide which one tae tak'."

"But you must have been there a hundred times," said Ollie.

"Richt ye are. But that's when I can tak' my time. Hae a look at the map in the glove box," said Wilma to Dr. Broth, who was sitting in the passenger's seat, "Ye see? The tolls're fur various amounts. An what's mair, some o' the roads're tolled both ways, others only in one direction. If I tak' as much time as I need, then I can avoid all the tollbooths, as ye can see."

"Oh sure, sure," said Dr. Broth.

"I can see that there's one way to avoid any tolls," said Ollie, looking over Dr. Broth's shoulder at the map, "but that's not necessarily the cheapest way to go. How many miles to the gallon do you get?"

"Ten kilometres tae the litre," said Wilma.

"And how much is gas here?"

"Fifty pence a litre."

"At that rate," said Ollie, "there's only one path to take to spend the least amount of money, though you will go through some tollbooths."

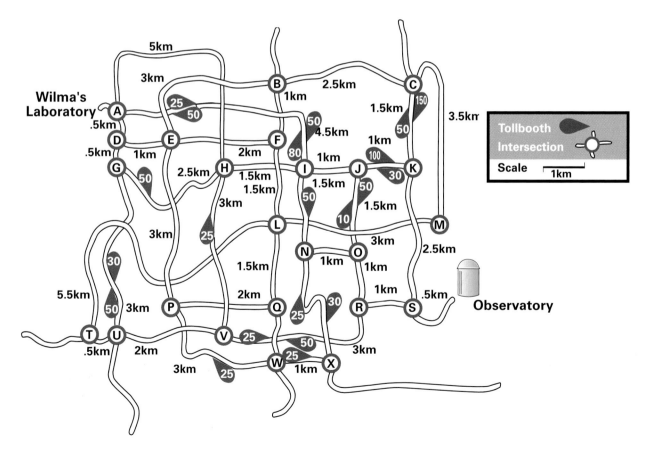

"But right now it's crucial that we get there as fast as possible, regardless of expense," said Dr. Broth.

"Well, assuming that every tollbooth adds an additional two minutes to the journey, what with slowing down, paying the toll, and having to accelerate again, there's really only one path to take."

"And if you factor in the time it takes to decide how to make a journey before we even start the car," said an irritated alpaca, "I'm fairly certain we'll never get anywhere."

Crash Pad

AS SOON AS THEY arrived at the observatory, they jumped out of the car and climbed a small hill to Tycho Braveheart's telescope. Wilma introduced them to the astronomer, a short, jolly, bearded man with a seeming glint in his eye. Upon further inspection the glint turned out to be the shine from his well-polished nose. Tycho hurried them inside and pressed a few buttons. A slit in the roof appeared. He turned the telescope and focused it toward the airport.

"Yes, yes, there's only one plane circling," he said, his patchy red beard parting to reveal a mouth. He seemed excited to be able to use his equipment to help them. "That must be it. Must be, must be. Here, take a look."

Tycho climbed out of the observer's chair and beckoned Dr. Broth over.

"Oh, yes, I see," said Dr. Broth, "it certainly seems to be going around and around. Reminds me of a . . . oh, no!" He began to shake. "Oh, oh, oh."

"What's the matter?" asked McGuffin.

"That plane. The plane with my briefcase on it seems to have just . . . to have just exploded."

"What!" shouted Tycho, scooting Dr. Broth out of the chair so that he could have a look for himself. The parachutes of the pilot and copilot billowed in the air. "You're right!" said Tycho. "Look . . . at . . . that . . . ."

Dr. Broth paced the floor of the observatory in a panic. "Random Highlanders will

soon be plowing under the pages of my manuscript."

Ollie, McGuffin, and Dr. Broth looked at the floor solemnly.

"After all we've gone through . . . ," said Ollie.

"For nothing," said McGuffin.

"A tairble shem," said Wilma.

Dr. Broth was too choked up to speak.

"Wait a bit," said Tycho from the observer's chair, "I think . . . I think I see something, something brown hurtling into space."

"Hurtling into space?" squeezed out Dr. Broth. "Must have been quite an explosion."

"Yes, yes. It looks quite like a briefcase. Judging by its trajectory and velocity, I'd say it's headed for, let's see, yes it's headed straight for Mercury. Straight for Mercury."

"That hardly helps matters," said Dr. Broth.

"On the contrary. I've been planning a trip to Mercury for years now. I've got a rocket out back, and everything's ready to go."

"How convenient," said McGuffin.

"There's just one small problem I have to work out with the robot, actually," added Tycho. "Wee beggars don't do what they're told."

They spilled out of the observatory, down the hill, and into a yard behind the lab. A giant rocket stood in the center of a series of concentric circles, each of which was divided into black or white subsections. A square or circle was inscribed in the middle of each section. A robot scurried around the perimeter. The lifeless hulls of nine other robots rested on various circles and squares.

"That robot," said Tycho, pointing to the only moving one, "still has to get to the rocket to adjust the oxygen valve. Unfortunately, all the robots seem to have a software bug. They can approach the rocket only in a straight line, and certain sequences of shapes and/or color cause them to self-destruct. I'm not sure if I can get the last robot to the rocket. I don't know what the sequences are that make the poor things expire. It's a real pain in the petunia!"

"The programming," started Dr. Broth, "must be very complex and yet very exact in order to carry out so many functions. If all the robots have the same program, I don't see how this one would be able to do what the others couldn't."

"That may be true," said Ollie, "but I think I can see which three sequences of shapes and colors are destroying the robots. And there's one path the remaining robot can take to avoid self-destructing."

Jumping Ahead

WORKING ALL BY ITSELF, the robot took a few days to repair the spaceship for departure and build a special alpaca space chair. When all the booster rockets were filled, all the O-rings in place, the coolant checked, and every screw given an extra twist, everyone climbed on board. They waved good-bye to Wilma, who had to attend to his clones.

Tycho strapped Ollie, Dr. Broth, and McGuffin into their seats and then called out to the robot, "Rudder!"

"Check," said the robot.

"Flaps!"

"Check."

"Ignition!" shouted Tycho.

"Check."

McGuffin leaned his head out the window.

"Pastrami!" he shouted.

"Check," said the robot.

"Hey, this is fun," said McGuffin. "Avocado!"

"Check."

"You're a mindless automaton!" hollered McGuffin.

Ready for Blast-off

"And you're a stinking, hairy, foulmouthed ruminant!" answered the robot.

McGuffin yanked his head back in. "Er, I guess we're ready for takeoff."

Tycho pushed a few blinking buttons. They heard a great roar, and suddenly the rocket was tearing through the air, squashing them against their chairs. When they'd burst through every layer of the atmosphere, the rocket stopped accelerating and the pressure eased. The seat-belt light above each of their chairs went off, and they were allowed to move about the cabin.

"Haven't had a massage like that in a long time," said McGuffin.

"It was interesting to see a demonstration of supersonic motion through a turbulent gas," said Dr. Broth.

"It's a long way to Mercury, a long, long way," said Tycho. "Anyone in the mood for a game of Variable Nebulaese Checkers?"

"Do the Variable Nebulitians play a lot of games?" asked Dr. Broth. "I was under the impression that they were a stoic bunch."

"You're right, of course. The Mercurians invented it thirty centuries ago, but they wanted to give the game an exotic sound, make it a little fancylike. So they named it after the Variable Nebula. It's very much like Chinese checkers, except each person only has four pieces and it's played on this hexagonal board of hexagons."

Tycho found the board, tucked away in one of the spaceship's junk drawers, and put it on the table. "Naturally, we use magnets instead of marbles. Each player's four pieces start in the corner in a Y formation. Everyone takes a turn moving a piece, and you can jump as much as you like during a single turn. The object is to get your pieces, in the same formation, to the opposite corner."

DR. BROTH AND MCGUFFIN were a little bored after the three hundredth odd game of Variable Nebulaese Checkers. Neither had won a single game.

"As much as I'm enjoying this," said Dr. Broth, "I really should do some thinking about my next project on the history of organic spatial craniology."

"Me too," said McGuffin.

A few days later Ollie and Tycho were once again placing their pieces to battle each other. Tycho hesitated before making his first move in their 132nd two-player game.

"It's getting harder and harder to stump you, my friend. I see a way to move both our pieces to their opposite sides in exactly sixteen moves. Can you figure that out?" he asked.

Ollie examined the board and then calmly executed the sixteen moves.

A Mercurial Etherforce

"YOU KNOW," SAID MCGUFFIN, tired of twiddling his hoofs, "I could take us there in a fraction of a second. I don't know why we're in this lunch box."

"You could take us *somewhere* in a fraction of a second," corrected Ollie.

Outside in the distance they could see eleven ships in formation, flying in the same direction as they were.

"That's the mighty Mercurian Etherforce," said Tycho. "They always fly in formations based on a hexagonal grid. You can see it on my screen here."

The spaceships appeared on the screen in front of Tycho's chair. "Those ships can fire in any of the six directions. They're set up so that they can cover every hexagon on the perimeter of the grid."

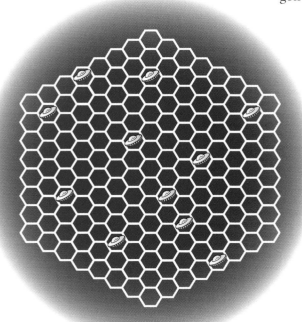

"In their current formation," pointed out Dr. Broth, "they can be sure they won't hit one another when they fire."

Suddenly four of the spaceships took off on a scouting mission.

"That ruins their entire setup!" said McGuffin.

"Actually," said Ollie, "the remaining seven ships can still fire without hitting one another and cover every hexagon in the grid if they arrange themselves correctly."

Touching Base on Mercury

SOON THE LITTLE PLANET Mercury was in their sights, a tiny floater on the eye of the sun.

"See the line where the light meets the dark?" asked Tycho. "That's where we're headed. The side of Mercury closest to the sun is molten hot at 840 degrees and would fry us in a matter of seconds. The other side, however, is ice-cold. Well, colder than that: dry ice–cold. Actually it's even colder than dry ice–cold. Really, really, cold dry ice–cold is probably more like it. Negative 300 degrees, if you must know. We've got to land right on the line between the two climates if we want to have a chance at surviving. Right on the line."

"But Mercury rotates once every fifty-eight and two-thirds Earth days during a yearly revolution of just eighty-eight Earth days. As a result of the rotation being such a large portion of the revolution, the time from dawn to dawn on Mercury is 176 Earth days," said Dr. Broth. "That strip of ideal temperature is always changing."

"You're right. We'll just have to stay on the move. It's to our advantage anyway. We can slowly circle the planet, looking for your luggage."

Mercury began to grow larger and larger in their window. For a moment it seemed as though they might crash, but Tycho slammed on the brakes just in time. As soon as they'd landed, they heard a strange clamor outside. They opened the door to find a crowd of creatures surrounding the spaceship. Strange beings of varying size, limb number, and eyeball count held signs that read, WELCOME, DR. BROTH. The crew stood dumbfounded at the door of the ship until a spokesbeing climbed up the steps to greet them. What appeared to be his assistants rolled out a red carpet from the foot of the rocketship through the crowd.

"Welcome to Mercury's 4,532nd annual intergalactic non-Euclidean paleolinguistic astrohistoriographical convention," said the spokesbeing. "We've all been waiting for the day when the distinguished Dr. Broth could attend."

A Mercurian Greeting

He reached out a hand toward the alpaca.

"Um, he's the wise guy," said McGuffin with a nod toward Dr. Broth.

"I'm dreadfully sorry," said the spokesbeing, who grasped Dr. Broth's hand and gave it a shake. "You know, all you Earthlings look so much alike." He marched them through the throng. They arrived at an enormous convention center that moved on giant tracks, and were seated close to the stage. Dr. Broth was hurried away to prepare for his awaited presentation.

"It's all so exciting," said Ollie. "It's good to know that Dr. Broth's work really is valuable."

"Or that the whole galaxy is filled with idiots," said McGuffin.

"I think McGuffin may be right," said Tycho, elbowing Ollie. "Look at that chalkboard behind the stage. The equations don't make any sense."

$$4\_4 = 10 \text{ in base } \_\_\_\_$$
$$6\_2 = 10 \text{ in base } \_\_\_\_$$
$$8\_2 = 10 \text{ in base } \_\_\_\_$$

30 or 36 or 26 or 1E

"Are they multiplying or adding?" asked McGuffin.

"Either way, two fours can't make ten. The answers are still wrong. Still wrong."

"Still wrong, still wrong?" asked McGuffin.

"Aye, aye," said Tycho, "still wrong, still wrong."

Ollie stared at the board for a few moments.

"You really should give them the benefit of the doubt," said Ollie. "Several creatures, each with a different number of fingers than we have, probably wrote those equations. Each equation seems to work as two different bases, depending on what you put in the blank as an operator. However, there's only one combination of bases that, added together, gives you the numbers at the bottom."

Introductory Remarks

SOON THE LIGHTS DIMMED and the murmur of intergalactic chatter died down. A spotlight fell on the stage, illuminating the spokesbeing in a seventeen-sleeved sports coat—with patches on every elbow. He walked up to the microphone-crammed podium and gave a little cough before beginning his speech. "Fellow beings from every corner of the universe, you cannot imagine how overjoyed I am to open the 4,532nd symposium on paleo—excuse me?"

"We can't hear you!" came shouts from the back of the auditorium.

The spokesbeing fiddled with some cords and tapped on the microphones. A squeal of feedback shot through the room. Multifarious fingers plugged multifarious ears. The spokesbeing gave another little cough.

"Is that better?"

"No!" came the shouts from the back.

Eventually a tiny furless ball wearing a utility belt rolled up to the stage and replaced several microphones.

"Please, excuse the delay," said the spokesbeing clearly. The audience settled. "To continue . . . today is a great day because this is the first time that we've been lucky enough to have a representative from Earth at our conference. Though not generally recognized as a leader in academic pursuits, Earth's current generation of non-Euclidean paleolinguistic astrohistoriographists has produced the brilliant and widely recognized Dr. Broth. Grateful we are to have him here today. So, without further ado, please give a hand, flipper, slab of flesh, or what have you, to the esteemed professor himself."

A din of slaps, clangs, whistles, what sounded like a slurred grunt, and a few belches greeted the professor who stumbled into the spotlight.

"Thank you, thank you. Ladies, Gentlemen, and so on, you're very kind, very kind. I haven't had much time to prepare, so I thought I'd talk a little about what I think to be the greatest problem facing non-Euclidean paleolinguistic astrohistoriographists today. Aside, that is, from the disappearance of my manuscript."

An alien sitting next to Ollie began transcribing Dr. Broth's every word as the doctor launched into his speech.

"The Hyde-body eigenvalues signify elemental linear insights. Gravitationally holistic text saturates Archean relativism. Elevating holism obviates thermocouple mysticism yielding tertiary Hyde-body results. Objects alienate text. Inertia sustains deconstructive registers. Yugawaralite initiates nucleosynthetic entropy. Eocene dematerialization semioticizes osmotic meme-worship. Eventually, worship annihilates tertiary eigenvector registration."

Ollie and McGuffin woke up to the clamor of applause.

Dr. Broth concluded his lecture, shouting hoarsely, "I repeat! Worship annihilates tertiary eigenvector registration!"

"I think Dr. Broth is trying to tell us something," said Tycho.

Questionable Answer Session

"ARE THERE ANY QUESTIONS?" Dr. Broth asked the audience.

A barbed and scaly hand shot up in the front row.

"Yes?" asked Dr. Broth over the continuing noisy hubbub.

"Do you feel there's any evidence to the claim that the inaccuracies of the thermocouple are to blame for Horsendrog's induplicable—and in my opinion, indefensible—conclusions of two millennia ago that have thrown off so much subsequent research?"

Dr. Broth looked down at the podium and pulled at his chin.

"Not really. Any other questions?"

A spindly creature with a bony goatee caught the professor's attention. "A recent study suggests that Glaxorab's constant may, in fact, be only partially invariant, limiting its usefulness to many types of kinship equations. Do you think this exciting new result will reshape research priorities?"

"Probably not. Anyone else?"

This time an oozing yellow tentacle rose a few rows in front of Ollie and McGuffin.

"Yes?" asked Dr. Broth.

"Could you put the words *Acorn, Astor, Elect, Gecko, Hater, Lilac, Mules,* and *Pluto* into two separate five-by-five word squares so that each word square reveals an extra word as of yet unstated?"

Dr. Broth looked down at the podium and pulled at his chin.

"I'll give you a hint," said the voice of the slimy tentacled being, "the missing words are something from *A* to *Z*."

Dr. Broth continued to pull at his chin, but he was now looking frantically through the audience.

"Eh, er, I'll have to consult my assistant on this one. We did some research a while back, but it seemed such a trivial matter at the time that I just filed it away. Oh, there he is."

Ollie quietly made his way down the aisle and handed Dr. Broth the results, which the doctor scratched out on the blackboard. Bitter arguments had broken out regarding the Hyde-body eigenvalues . . .

Three Feet Wide and Rising

HOURS LATER, AFTER EVERYONE had dispersed, the spokesbeing gave Tycho and the trio a tour of the fantastic convention center grounds.

"One thing I don't understand," said Ollie, "is how everyone lives here. I thought that one side of Mercury was too hot for life and the other too cold."

"You come from a planet with such a restricted range of climates," said the spokesbeing. "The Mercurians have adapted to a much more diverse planet. That's one of the great engineering feats they've pulled off. Most of the creatures at this convention, you realize, are not from Mercury."

"Who are the Mercurians?" asked McGuffin.

"They're the round ones that organize everything. They've actually fixed up this planet quite nicely. Millions of years ago they were simple spherical clusters of cells that had evolved to roll forever west so as to stay in the temperate strip between the warm and cold. Eventually their technology evolved with them, and they built roads around the planet to make rolling easier. Today, this entire convention center circles the globe on gigantic tracks that have replaced the roads. Those ingenious gumballs—that's what we Lagoon Nebulans call them—raised the roads three feet and put all the machinery under it. Some kind of magnetic system, I believe."

"How on Earth, er, in the world, did they raise the roads?" asked Dr. Broth.

The spokesbeing stopped near a spherical lamp. He bent down and undid one of his many shoelaces. He wrapped the shoelace around the equator of the lamp.

"See, this lamp has a circumference of thirty inches. If we add about twenty inches to the shoelace, we can raise it three inches off the face of the lamp—that is, add six inches to its diameter. Do you have any idea," said the spokesbeing, turning to Dr. Broth, "how much road the Mercurians would have to add to raise it three inches off the planet? The road goes around the equator, the diameter of which is 3,032 miles."

"I'm afraid that's not my area of expertise," said Dr. Broth.

"I think I have an idea," said Ollie.

Rolling Rats

"I'D LIKE YOU TO meet a colleague of mine," said the spokesbeing as they walked into a building named Hermes Hall. "Though he is a non-Euclidean paleolinguistic astrohistoriographist, he specializes in the social life of Mercurial rodents."

He led them into a sterile white room. In the center was an enormous cube standing on one of its corners. Each of the three sides that faced them was a maze covered with a sheet of glass. A clean-cut being with thick glasses examined a surface of the cube, a pencil in one hand, a clipboard in the other, a calculator in yet another, a tape measure in yet another, a magnifying glass in yet another, and a bag marked Feed in yet another. He scratched his head with a seventh hand.

"Ray Rodento, I'd like you to meet some of the brightest folks in the universe," said the spokesbeing,

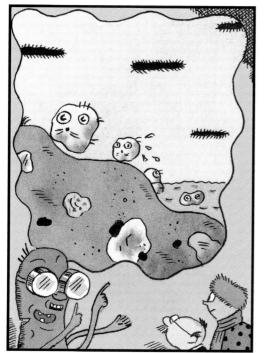

Ball Rat Evolution

"Ollie, Dr. Broth, McGuffin, Tycho, meet Dr. Ray Rodento, Mercury's leading naked ball-rat scholar. He's from the Hamster Nebula himself." Everyone shook hands with Dr. Rodento—all at once.

Rodento launched right into his research. "Today's Mercurians are descended from creatures very much like these ball rats. Back in the Moleozoic era the seminaked ball rat—close relative of the ball rats you see here—was the most advanced life-form on the planet. The Moleozoic rodents differ only in size, the length of their tibiae, and eyesight. These rats here are nearly blind, but their ancestors, most likely, could see as well as you or I."

He turned back to the cube and knocked his face against the glass.

As Dr. Rodento recovered, the others moved in for a closer look at the naked ball rats. Under the glass, fleshy little spheres rolled through the maze, some of them pushing other little spheres that looked like bits of food.

"I see that these creatures have quite a sophisticated social structure," remarked Dr. Broth. "There are scouts who look for food, workers who collect and distribute the food, warriors who protect the queen, taxi drivers, skate rats, mall rats, and writers who spend the day in coffee shops. What is it you're studying?"

"Right now we're testing their intelligence and sense of smell. We've put several pieces of Edam cheese in the corner of the maze marked with a red dot. Then we put a ball rat in the corner marked with the blue dot—it's also their dining room. As close as they are to the cheese, they can't get to it without going through the maze first. Tunnels in the cube lead from one face of the maze to another. Any two points marked with the same letter are connected by a tunnel. We haven't found a rat that can do it yet!" said Dr. Rodento proudly.

"Nor an alpaca, I'll bet," said McGuffin as he stared at the maze confusedly.

"I'll trace it out for you, if you'd like," said Ollie.

Return to Sender

"I'VE BEEN TOLD," SAID the spokesbeing, "that on your planet creatures are sensitive to small fluctuations in climate and weather."

"Seasons," said McGuffin, "it gives the humans something to talk about."

"And that the population of your life-form," continued the spokesbeing with a nod to the humans present, "is split into different temperature zones, depending on age."

"And economic status," said Dr. Broth.

"And so it is on Mercury. In their constant progression around the planet, those insulated with sufficient blubber tend to move toward the front, whereas the elderly and the rich usually follow on the warmer side toward the sun."

"They're behind us now?" asked Ollie.

"That's correct. The Mercurian youth are forever followed by geezers in Bermuda shorts."

Suddenly Dr. Broth looked as if he'd just remembered something.

"This is all very interesting," he said, "but the reason we came here, er, one of the reasons, was to find my missing manuscript, which was headed your way."

"Was it in a briefcase?"

"Why, yes."

"A brown, overstuffed briefcase?"

"Yes, yes, that's it."

"We sent that back on the first flight of the interplanetary bookmobile. It left on Monday."

BACK IN THE SPACESHIP Tycho was apologizing for the unsuccessful trip. "But at least we know that it's safely on its way back," he said.

"We forgot to ask where on Earth the bookmobile's going," said Dr. Broth.

"I think they're trying to tell us right now," said Ollie, looking out the window. Beneath them the Mercurians had arranged themselves into six rectangles, each with dark and light sections.

"They just haven't got the right formation yet," said Ollie. "With a few turns and a little overlapping, our destination is spelled out."

Seventy Million Miles to Home

THE TRAVELERS WERE DISCUSSING how to pass the time on their long space flight back to Earth.

"I've never even won a game of regular chess," said McGuffin. "You can't expect me to be able to play a three-D version."

"I'll give you a little exercise to practice with while we play," said Tycho. "On this four-by-four-by-four board, a knight must move two spaces horizontally and one space vertically, or one space horizontally and two spaces vertically. Try to capture the rook, bishop, queen, and king, and then return to the spot from which you started—all in eight moves. No less, no more."

While McGuffin toiled away at the problem, Ollie demolished Tycho in a full game.

"I'm amazed, amazed," said Tycho, trying to distract Ollie with conversation, "at your incredible abilities with languages. I knew, of course, from your stories that you've more than gotten by in Moscow and the distant future. But the fact that each of you could understand Plutonium, Andromedanese, the northern dialects of NGC 6781, and Regulsian, really . . . well, it's astounding. Although you didn't do too well with the Uranians, but maybe that was just because of their heavy crater-creature accent. That aside, you chaps really proved yourselves the polyglots. How do you do it?"

"Alpacas," said Ollie, "from having to survive in so many different worlds and times, have evolved an incredible language instinct. We humans may have the rules of syntax programmed into our heads, but every alpaca is born with a complete vocabulary."

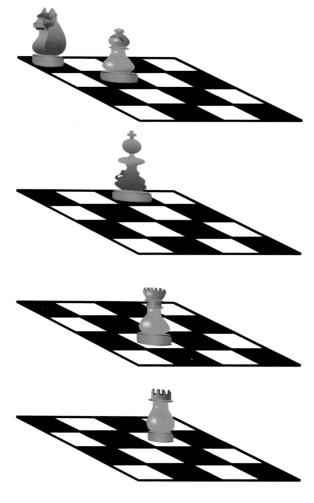

"But languages evolve, too," said Tycho. "A word can change to mean its complete opposite in the period of a century."

"And alpacas have been to those centuries," said Ollie.

"Ollie, however, just had the good luck to grow up in a multiethnic Brooklyn neighborhood," said McGuffin.

"And you, Doctor?" Tycho asked.

"I've spent my life studying a full range of languages, from Khoisan to Krio. My understanding of the generative grammar allows me to adapt to any kind of speech. I'm at the point now where mere syntactic atoms aren't really an issue. Despite the odd listeme, I can almost always figure out what someone's trying to say from the context."

After a few more moves, Tycho threw down his pieces and smacked his forehead.

"I can't take you to where you're going! The air regulations won't permit it. I have to land back at my observatory. I'm afraid you'll have to try to catch up with your bag some other way."

"Should we risk traveling with McGuffin again?" Ollie asked Dr. Broth, who merely shrugged his shoulders.

As soon as Earth emerged from the blackness, they were off again on McGuffin's back.

Fast-Fold Restaurant

"IT DOESN'T SEEM POSSIBLE," Dr. Broth said in amazement.

"What doesn't seem possible?" asked the alpaca.

"This appears to be the New York I left. You've actually done it for once. You've brought us to the place and time we wanted to go to."

"The place and time *you* wanted to go to," said McGuffin, "I was hoping to catch Gypsy Rose Lee at the Irving Place Theater in the 1930s."

"I wouldn't have minded a chance to see Babe Ruth . . . ," said Ollie wistfully.

"Then I guess I just got lucky," said the doctor. He crossed the intersection to a pay phone and called the airport. From across the street, Ollie and McGuffin watched a more or less happy Doctor Broth become confused, frustrated, and then dejected. With the phone between his ear and shoulder, he gesticulated, making rectangles in the air with parallel hands. Ollie and McGuffin could just make out the words *leather, handle,* and *flapdoodle* on his lips.

He hung up the phone and returned to the curious pair.

"My briefcase hasn't arrived yet," he said. "We're three years too early."

They stared at the ground.

"Any chance you could jump ahead another three years?" said Ollie.

"Well, I'm really hungry. Know any Burger Burlesques?" McGuffin asked Dr. Broth.

"I do not. Not too far from here, however, is an excellent restaurant I once frequented years ago—I mean around this time—I believe a reformed gambler and country musician opened it. Sadly, it went out of business after a few months. Now would be a great opportunity to eat there again."

Soon they were chewing overcooked roast chicken at Lenny Codger's on Thirteenth and Sixth. Ollie and McGuffin looked at each other incredulously as Dr. Broth ravished his sandwich.

"Wasn't that delicious?" asked the doctor as he gulped down the last bite and prepared to leave.

"Never had anything like it," said the alpaca noncommittally. He scribbled a few letters on a napkin and slid it across the counter before they left.

"How will anyone understand that?" whispered Ollie as they stepped out the door.

"I hope the owner gets it," said McGuffin. "If he folds it so the letters stack up right, he'll get my message."

A Volume Discount

"IF WE'RE GOING TO BE SPENDING so much time wandering all over the universe, I'd like to take care of something I wish I'd done before we left," said Dr. Broth.

"What? Hide your diary or pay your overdue fines at the library?" asked McGuffin.

"If I'd known we were going to be gone for so long, I would have sublet my apartment. Just think of all the money I've been throwing away on rent. And since I've got you two, packing up will be a lot easier."

"Aaargh! The greatest curse of acquaintanceship," cried McGuffin.

As they wandered through the streets toward Dr. Broth's apartment, Ollie and McGuffin trailed as far behind the doctor as possible, hoping to escape. Dr. Broth had to frequently glance back to keep them securely tethered with the bonds of guilt.

The doctor's apartment was a seven-story walkup on Fourth Street. Ollie and McGuffin groaned with every step as they climbed the narrow stairs. Dr. Broth unlocked his door and ushered the pair into an apartment filled entirely with books and dust.

"*Pthhhhhpt,*" let out the alpaca.

"Llama?" said the doctor. "Did I say *llama*?"

"That was a sneeze. What are you planning to do with all that dust?"

Dr. Broth was already putting books in boxes. "With three people, this'll be done in no time. Jon Arburg's theory of mass production states that as the head count of an industry unit rises, productivity increases more than that number simply multiplied. Up to a point, of course, up to a point. I can't quite remember the exact formula, but

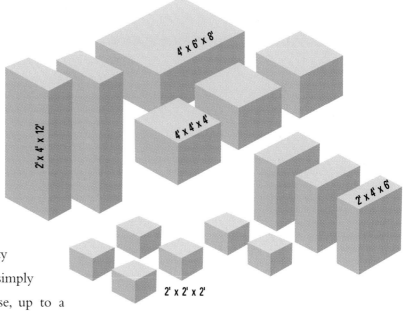

with three people instead of one, I think we should be able to finish this job in about twenty-eight-hundredths of the time it would take for me to do it alone."

"I think you're forgetting to factor in the possibility that if one of those counted heads happens to be spouting drivel, he might bore the others to sleep, reducing productivity to a standstill." With that the alpaca sat on his haunches.

Hours later Ollie and Dr. Broth piled fifteen heavy boxes onto McGuffin's back and marched him a few blocks west to Stuff It! Self Storage. There they rented an eight-by-eight-by-twelve-foot room.

Dr. Broth scratched his head as they looked at the pile of boxes near the door. "I know we should be able to fit them in here, but I just can't see how. Maybe we should just pile them right back on the alpaca and take them home. I'll take a little off the rent for a subletter willing to live with the boxes."

"An unwise decision," spat McGuffin.

"Oh, I think I see a way to fit everything inside," said Ollie.

Just as they fit the last box into their Stuff It! Self Storage space, a female attendant ran up to them.

"Excuse me, excuse me," she said, "we need this refrigerated room to store the Museum of Modern

Ice's sculpture collection for the summer. Would you mind moving to another room? It has the same volume, but it's an eight-by-six-by-sixteen-foot space."

"I don't know how we could fit all this stuff in there. It barely fits with these dimensions," said Dr. Broth.

"Actually, there is a way to fit everything in the other room just as easily," said Ollie.

Window of the Soul

THEY WERE SITTING AROUND several pizza boxes on the floor of the barren apartment, trying to word a classified ad for the place, when they heard a key slip into the lock of the door.

Dr. Broth leapt up, ran to the closet and reappeared with a baseball bat as the key slid out of the handle lock and another slid into the bolt. The doctor tiptoed toward the door, making circles of anticipation with the bat. The door flew open.

The two men facing each other looked very much alike.

"What the—" they said simultaneously.

"It's the Dr. Broth from three years ago. Er, eh—I guess it's our Dr. Broth that's from the future," whispered Ollie to McGuffin, "and look: they both have the same tweed jackets with elbow patches."

"How long has he been wearing that thing?" McGuffin wondered out loud.

"I can't tell for sure," said Ollie. "The only difference between them seems to be that where our Dr. Broth is wielding a baseball bat, the other is carrying one bulging brown attaché case!"

"What are you doing in my apartment?" demanded the two Dr. Broths.

Then Dr. Broth noticed the briefcase. With a whoop, he threw the bat aside and made a dive for it. The other Broth was too astonished to move and only emitted a low decibel *"eep."*

"Thank heavens! I've found it!" shouted Dr. Broth. He popped open the clasps and yanked out the papers. As he thumbed through them, his face grew redder and redder.

"These pages are blank! What's happened?"

"I'm sorry, very sorry. I didn't know anyone was watching me," said the doctor, "I'll give them back. I . . . I . . . it was just more convenient than having to go out and buy my own. I was hoping—"

A look of recognition, then recollection crossed the doctor's face. "Oh yes, how could I forget?" said the doctor. "Years ago—today, I guess—I decided to finally start putting all my notes together and begin

An Awkward Entry

work on my book. So I . . . uh, borrowed a ream of paper from the office."

The newly arrived Dr. Broth suddenly snapped out of his apologetic state. "Who are you? What are you doing in my apartment pretending to be me?"

"Pretending to be you? It's I that is me, not you. You're the impostor."

"It's certainly possible, with all the time traveling we've done, that you're both Dr. Broth," said Ollie. "Isn't there something we can do to prove it?"

"Time traveling?" asked the new arrival. He pointed to the M-shaped window of the apartment. "If you're me, you ought to be able to divide the triangle on the left side of the window into eleven smaller right triangles, all of which have legs with a two-to-one ratio, six of which are identical. Without ruining any of the left side's triangles, you should be able to divide the triangle on the right into ten triangles with a ratio of two to one, all of which are a unique size."

"Seeing as how I've lain in that bed for years, dividing the window in just such a manner, that'll be no problem at all," said the elder Dr. Broth. The two of them grabbed a piece of the blank, contraband paper and went to separate corners to sketch out their answers.

Restoring Order

AFTER THEY'D MADE UP and Dr. Broth explained everything to Dr. Broth, the quartet caught the D train up to the Bronx for a Yankee game. Ollie insisted on box seats. McGuffin had a hotdog and a beer, while the Broths stuck to popcorn and lemonade.

As they waited for the game to start, Ollie noticed that Dr. Broth the elder seemed rather distraught. "Don't worry," consoled Ollie, "we'll find your briefcase sooner or later."

"Yes," said the doctor, still distracted, "it's just that I've never seen myself from behind. I had no idea my head was so bald."

IT WAS GETTING LATE and the game hadn't begun.

A middle-aged man in a pinstriped uniform sat next to Ollie and put his arm around his shoulder.

"Boy, am I glad you're here, Ollie. I thought you were out of town for a few weeks. Missed you at the game last night," said the man.

"Why, hello, Joe. Somehow I managed to find the time for tonight's ball game. What's the holdup?"

"I just can't figure out the batting order. I've been running around in circles."

"What seems to be the problem?"

"The boss made a big trade last night. Not only do I have a handful of new players, but he also traded away all our designated hitters."

"So the pitcher's got to hit ninth?"

"That's right, Ollie. But it gets more complicated. Gomez always hits in the first inning."

"As usual. Must be in his contract."

"Douglas wants to be behind Heap but ahead of Iverson."

"Gotta keep 'em happy."

"No outfielder should hit later than sixth."

"I've always agreed with you there."

"Shortstop second."

"Right."

"Benitez is in center field, Archer on second base."

"Of course. That's where they've played their entire careers."

"Cooper can play either catcher or first base."

"That's a little unusual."

"If Fitzgerald gets a hit, then Heap should come to bat. If Earl gets a hit, Archer should come to bat."

"Sound strategy."

"Iverson hits seventh, of course."

"His lucky number."

"The right fielder should hit in the first inning. And the first baseman has to hit cleanup."

"Keep the strong ones up front."

"Double plays usually go Gomez to Archer to Douglas. And the second baseman should hit sixth—just a superstition of mine."

"So what seems to be the problem?"

"Well, I can't make it all work."

"Actually, there's only one way it can work."

The Copper Con

OUTSIDE, AFTER THE GAME, a small crowd had gathered around a man with a table that had been made by placing a piece of cardboard over two boxes. He was sliding a penny between three walnut shells.

"Where's the penny, where's the penny, where's the penny, cute little penny? That's all you gotta tell me: Which shell's got the penny, shiny little penny? Anybody can do it, anybody. Where's the penny, where's the penny, where's the penny? That man over there in the golf cap just walked away with two hundred dollars. Gonna buy himself a baseball card. Who's next? Where's the penny, where's the penny, where's the penny?"

The eyes of the crowd went back and forth, following the penny from shell to shell. Suddenly, the shells froze, and the man behind the makeshift table stopped talking. A woman in the front row gave her little girl a five-dollar bill.

Fleeing from the Fuzz

"That one, that one!" shouted the girl, pointing to the shell on the left.

The man lifted the middle and left shell simultaneously. The mischievous penny sat under the middle one.

"Sorry, kid," said the man, snatching the five dollars. The money disappeared into a pocket, and the penny shuttled once more from shell to shell.

"Where's the penny, where's the penny, where's the penny, shiny little penny, she's a cute little penny . . ."

By now the time travelers and the extra Dr. Broth had moved to the front row.

"This is just a case of Slowdinger's moose," said Dr. Broth the elder. "In the quantum realm, at any given nanosecond, that penny, or portions of it, can be at two places at the same time. And given that the observer's continuous attention is shaping the penny's existence from event to event—"

"—the penny's quarks reassemble approximately h-bar k-naught seconds after the observer selects a shell," said the other doctor, finishing the sentence of the first.

"Just tell me where the penny is. That's the game—in a nutshell," shouted the huckster. And again the shells lay motionless.

The two Dr. Broths each had a fifty in their hands. "The middle," they said.

The man raised the middle shell. Nothing was beneath it. Lifting the outer shells together he revealed the penny on the right. The doctors, one hundred dollars poorer, looked bewildered.

"Excuse me," said Ollie to the man. "I can't help noticing that the cardboard you're using has an interesting triangular pattern on it. I was wondering if you'd give me a chance to win my friends' money back with a different penny game."

"Double or nothing? How's it played?"

The crowd moved in a little tighter. Ollie took five more pennies from his pocket and placed them on the table, arranging the six coins in a circle. They alternated between heads and tails with one penny on each triangle.

"The rules are simple. A penny can slide across the side of a triangle and stay just as it is. If it moves to any triangle that it just touches at the point but is not adjacent, then it has to flip. All you have to do is move the pennies into an all-heads row in six moves or less. I'll give you two tries."

"You're on."

The man moved a few pennies, then frowned, moved a few more, then tucked his mouth into a low corner of his face. After a few minutes he looked up and pointed to a policeman, who'd been standing on the corner for the whole game.

"Cops! Gotta go," he barked as he knocked over the table and fled down the street.

A Bronx Tail

THE CON MAN'S SUDDEN diversionary disturbance and disappearance left the crowd without a center. People moved off in different directions. Mysteriously spooked, McGuffin tore off at a gallop. The two doctors and Ollie ran after him.

"What's the matter?" asked Ollie when they'd caught up with McGuffin.

"The police don't take kindly to camelids without a leash."

"Stop, you con artists!" came a shout from behind. McGuffin twisted his head to see the policeman in full pursuit.

"The fine for illegal games of chance is one thousand dollars and two weeks in jail," said one of the doctors between breaths. "Perhaps we should beat a hasty retreat."

They ran across the intersection beneath the elevated subway stop for the stadium. The heavyset policeman stopped running, bent over and tried to regain his breath. Then he spoke into his radio. "Three con men and one short, fuzzy, stray antelope fleeing the stadium." Several blocks away a police car's lights began to flash. The sound of its siren grew louder and louder as the car approached them. Nearby, an old lady was dragging a cartful of groceries into her apartment building. They rushed in before she could close the door behind her. Ollie offered her an apology as they bounded up the stairs two by two. The old woman quickly locked herself in her apartment. The foursome burst onto the roof just in time to see several police cars squeal to a halt in front of the building. The police hurried to the door and started smashing it with axes.

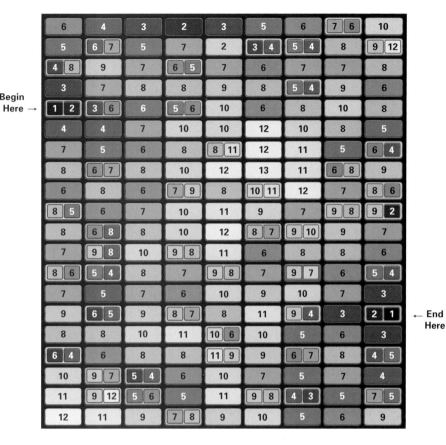

Begin Here →

← End Here

"Now what?" asked Ollie.

"I know a disguise store on Sixteenth and Third, but I don't know how we'd get there," said the younger Dr. Broth.

"I could probably jump from roof to roof, as long as I never have to jump diagonally or more than one story up or down," said McGuffin.

"Do you think it's possible to get there that way?" asked Ollie. The police had finished demolishing the door.

"I bought these today. Maybe they could help," said McGuffin. He handed Ollie a stack of postcards.

"Street shots of the Bronx?" asked Ollie.

"They were ten for a dollar," McGuffin said, "I couldn't turn down that kind of bargain."

Ollie quickly riffled through them as the sounds of heavy police steps came from the stairwell. Finding an aerial view among the postcards, he spent a moment studying it. The number of stories was indicated on each building.

"There's only one way there if you can only go up or down one story from building to building."

PUTTING ASIDE THEIR VIDEO cameras and removing their foam-rubber Lady Liberty hats, the time travelers shed their disguises and prepared themselves for departure. McGuffin felt confident that he could jump a mere thirty-six months into the future.

Astride McGuffin, Ollie waited for Dr. Broth the elder, who was having a last word with his double.

". . . and don't forget to tie the Dorians to ribosome forty-four, using the Arcam postulate. Too much of chapter three hinges on it to leave it out," he said.

"Oh yes, yes, of course. But it occurred to me just now that perhaps you really are better suited to the task, having written it once already. Based on your reports of McGuffin's inaccuracies, it may take so long to find the manuscript that it would be just as efficient to rewrite it. So, if one of us is going to be writing it anyway, it makes sense that you should be the one . . . ," said the second Dr. Broth.

"And you would be free to play Go in the park till your vertebrae fused, I suppose?"

"I'll simply continue where you left off. We can't both be here. Nor can we give up looking for the completed manuscript. And imagine my joy, if I should catch up with the attaché case. My life's work completed without my having so much as lifted a pencil. Economically, it makes sense."

The doctors reflected.

"I admit your argument seems flawless. My only concern is that you might seem a bit out of place at the office not having experienced the last three years, er, the three years to come."

"Has anything extraordinary, aside from writing the manuscript, happened in those years?"

"Not that I can think of."

"Have you made any wild purchases? New clothes, perhaps?"

"No."

"Have you got in any arguments, ticked anyone off?"

"You know me."

"Just making certain. People change, you never know. Have you actually met any new people?"

"I don't think so."

"That's not a worry," said McGuffin, "staring strangely at someone you ought to recognize won't seem odd to anyone that knows you."

"At least you'll get a few extra meals at Lenny Codger's," said Ollie.

In a trice, Ollie, McGuffin and the new Dr. Broth were attempting a three-year leap into the future, in search of the ever-elusive manuscript.

Backward Knights and Knaves

"I DON'T KNOW WHAT that old buffoon was complaining about," said the new Dr. Broth to McGuffin. "Not only did you get in here exactly on time, but we landed right in front of the baggage-claim counter."

The unclaimed-baggage clerk returned with his clipboard.

"Found out about your bag. The ground crew thought the chicken scratch on the tag was Japanese. They sent it on to Kyoto."

TOUCHING DOWN IN KYOTO the time travelers didn't find a runway. Instead, they appeared on a thin path between two fields.

A sign labeled Kyoto sent them in the right direction. But after a half mile or so, they came to a fork in the road. Each new path had its own sign also labeled Kyoto. Between these two signs sat two short grubby men in tatters sharing a bottle of saki under a tree.

"Greetings," said the more ragged of the two. "I suppose you're trying to get to Kyoto. I might as well tell you that one of these paths leads to the real Kyoto. . . ."

"And the other," said the slightly cleaner man, "leads to the Liars' Kyoto."

"One of us comes from the Kyoto of Liars, where everything anyone says is a lie."

"And one of us comes from the Kyoto of Truth-tellers, where everything anyone says is true."

"One of us is telling the truth."

"And one of us is telling nothing but lies."

"Can you guess which is—"

There was a rustle from above, then a flash and the glint of steel. A warrior in orange robes leapt out of a tree, slicing the air with two swords. At once the two grubby men sprang to their feet and fled. But before they could get very far, the man in orange had ripped open the remains of their clothes with a few sharp cuts. The ridiculous fellows ran away, their buttocks exposed for all to see.

Musashi Descends

"Knaves!" shouted the warrior after them. He came back along the path toward the trio, who were tripping over themselves trying to get out of his way.

"Oh, excuse me," said the man putting his swords back in their sheaths and giving them a bow. "My name is Musashi. I mean no harm. Those damn Liar/Truth-teller monkeys needed a lesson. No one wants to hear it from them anymore. Can I help you in any way?"

"Why, yes," said Dr. Broth, "could you tell us if we happen to have landed in an era of air travel?"

"The samurai Ganryu can hover in the air for what seems to be as long as he likes. But one must first master his spirit and body."

Dr. Broth threw a scowl over his shoulder at McGuffin.

"And when do we . . . er, can you tell me who the current shogun is?"

"Of course. Everyone knows it's Hidetada Tokugawa."

"That puts us in the early 1600s," said Dr. Broth with a knowing nod.

"Would you like me to accompany you to Kyoto? It's a dangerous path filled with many fools, scoundrels, and con men."

"We'd be very grateful," McGuffin piped in, hoping to get a chance to visit the red-light district.

As they approached Kyoto, Musashi turned to them.

"This evening I will be enjoying some of Kyoto's famous Non theater. Perhaps you'd care to join me."

"Oh, you probably mean the No theater," answered Dr. Broth. "*No* means 'skill,' I believe, and there are five different types of plays, the *kami*, a religious story about—"

"I'm sorry, but that's not what we'll be seeing tonight. I'm talking about the Non theater. Every line of every Non play is a palindrome. Sometimes they're quite clever. Often they're completely stupid, but they're always good old-fashioned samurai fun."

"What's tonight's performance?" Ollie asked eagerly.

"I think this one's called 'St. Ovid Made Dam Divots.' Don't ask me what it's about."

"Doesn't sound like one of the cleverer ones," said McGuffin.

They arrived at the theater just before it sold out. Musashi bought the last four tickets and handed them out to everyone.

"How many people can this theater seat?" asked Dr. Broth.

"One hundred and ninety-nine."

"That's odd," said Ollie, "my ticket says two hundred."

"At the Non theater," explained Musashi, "every seat number must be able to make a palindrome when added to the mirror image of that number. If that sum isn't a palindrome then it, too, must be added to its reflection. The process is repeated until a palindrome appears: 83 plus 38, for instance, makes

121, a palindromic number; 82 added to 28, however, makes 110. Since that number is not palindromic, just repeat the process: 110 and 011 make 121. So you see, 82 eventually becomes a palindrome. There's one number between one and two hundred though, that never becomes a palindrome, even if the process is repeated a million times. So there's no chair in the Non theater with that number."

Dr. Broth was already scratching additions into the dirt.

Ollie didn't say anything as he watched the doctor's calculations, but his face took on the slightest shade of smugness.

Rise U!? O.K. Ollie, Sir

THEY SEATED THEMSELVES IN the back of the theater. The lights dimmed and the curtain went up. The scene was late day at the beach. A few umbrellas, surfboards, sand castles, and weight machines littered the set. Actors dressed as a Minolta, a Canon, a Pentax, and an old Nikon came on stage. They wore very small bathing suits, and their arms and legs were bare. And they all had very large muscles. Great big vein-popping muscles. The actors began to flex and pose. Occasionally one would pick up some weights and do bicep curls, or lay on his back and bench-press a few hundred pounds.

Eventually a woman in a bikini appeared on the side of the stage. She looked at the other actors posing, flexing, and lifting weights. Then, as if overcome with excitement, she put her hands to her cheeks and said something in a sigh.

Dr. Broth leaned over to Ollie. "What did she say?" he asked.

"I'm not quite sure," said Ollie, grinning to himself. "It sounded like four words. Two letters in the first word, seven letters in the second, three letters in the third, and five in the last. There seemed to be a slight pause—maybe even a comma—between the first and second word. And, of course, it's the same forward and backward.

A Dada

THE CURTAIN WENT DOWN to a thunder of applause. After a lot of banging around on the stage, the curtain rose again. This time the set was bare except for a black cube in the center. An actor, in a suit of shells, came on stage and stood on top of the cube. He looked about contentedly. Then some actors in suits made of rocks and pebbles crept onto the stage. They twittered among themselves and slowly approached the center. The actor on the cube didn't notice them at first, but soon their chatter became too loud to ignore. They were looking at him, pointing at him and laughing. His look of contentedness disappeared. He began to twist inward, a look of anguish on his face. Soon the actors in the rock suits made a ring around him and openly mocked him. They called him Shellboy, and they laughed uproariously. The actor in the shells was contorting, trying to make himself as small as possible. One of the pebble actors seemed to be the ringleader. He pointed and laughed, pointed and laughed, and the others followed suit, emboldened by his brashness and cruelty.

Suddenly the actor on the platform had had enough. He stood up straight, pointed at the ringleader and shouted.

"I didn't catch that," said McGuffin, "what did he say?"

"Oh yes," said Ollie, "three words with four letters in the first, three in the second, and eight in the third. Perhaps there was a slight pause, this time between the second and third word. Another palindrome, naturally."

Piece of Cake

AFTERWARD, THEY WALKED THROUGH the Kyoto streets admiring the flower girls, fruit stalls, and all the construction that was going on.

"I hope you liked the play," said Musashi as they left the theater.

"Very moving," said Dr. Broth, "the submerging of the self, the homage to theater of the absurd, the aesthetic deployment of archaic icons in juxtaposition with neoplastic phalanx imagery were all well balanced in a superb amalgam. Shakespeare meets Brecht in a sushi bar run by Artaud, you might say."

Soon they reached a bridge where a crowd was chattering excitedly. When they saw Musashi approaching with the odd-looking foreigners, a hush passed through them and they parted to let him cross.

At the center of the bridge was a sign with Musashi's name scrawled across the top:

Musashi:

That wasn't very nice of you to kill half the members of the Okubyo school, even if it was in self-defense. They only wanted to kill you because you killed Tanaka. I know what you're thinking—that you only killed Tanaka because Tanaka challenged you. But Tanaka only challenged you because you killed Nobukazu. Yes, of course, you only killed Nobukazu because he challenged you in order to revenge Yamatsuka. And, it's true Yamatsuka was revenging Noriko. . . . It goes on like that for a while, but we both know YOU STARTED IT. Let's settle this once and for all. Meet us at the Okubyo school on July 23.

"That's today!" said Ollie.

"You're right," said Musashi. "Would you like to come?"

"I don't think you should go," said Ollie. "You might get hurt. It's obviously a trap. Besides, isn't it a little unfair for you to have to meet them at their school?"

"Don't worry about that. I can handle these clowns."

The Deciding Slice

WHEN MUSASHI, accompanied by the time travelers, knocked at the door of the Okubyo school that evening, a scared servant opened it with a bow and led them toward the dojo. Ollie and McGuffin looked around nervously, expecting swords to fall on them at any moment. Dr. Broth seemed to be admiring the architecture.

In the fighting room, seven samurai sat on the floor.

"Where's everyone else?" asked Musashi, rapidly approaching them.

"You killed them, don't you remember?" shouted the biggest of the group as they leapt to their feet. "Why the backup this time?"

"They're just here as witnesses."

A nearly inaudible sound filled the air, and in an instant all the samurai had their swords out.

A fraction of a second later, a bell rang, and the servant came in carrying a boysenberry shortcake on a tray.

"A samurai is a master of his mind and his body," said the leader of the Okubyo school. "If you're the great samurai you claim to be, cut that boysenberry shortcake into eight equal sections with only three cuts of the sword. You may not move any piece of the cake between cuts."

Musashi pondered the cake for a moment.

"And if I do?"

"Then we will admit defeat."

"But there won't be a piece for us," whined McGuffin.

A Troubled Bridge over Water

"WHAT WAS THAT?" SAID a startled Dr. Broth. "I thought I heard some butterflies whispering in my ear."

Ollie pointed toward the boysenberry shortcake, which was still on the servant's tray, which was still in the servant's hands. The cake looked the same but the servant was frozen with fear. Musashi brought his sword, still clean and gleaming, down from above his head and put it in its sheath.

"I don't understand," said Dr. Broth. "What happened? What's the matter?"

Musashi was leaning toward the boysenberry shortcake. When he was about two feet away, he gave a little puff, and a moment later, when the breath of wind had traveled from Musashi's lips to the tray, the cake fell apart into eight equal pieces.

The members of the school jumped toward the servant and began to hurl curses at him.

"Conspirator!" they shouted.

"You planned this!"

"We never saw his sword move!"

"He paid you!"

Musashi silenced them.

"You can bring me as many boysenberry shortcakes as you can make," he said calmly from outside the circle, "and they will all come to the same end."

"I wish they would bring as many boysenberry shortcakes as they can make," said McGuffin.

After everyone had had their fill of boysenberry shortcake (they did, in fact, bring another for Ollie and Dr. Broth, and a third for McGuffin) and the seven remaining members of the Okubyo school had sworn to devote their lives to the study of Musashi's Way of the Two Swords, the four friends left to find lodgings.

On their way they came to an archipelago. Three bridges connected two islets to the mainland. Unfortunately, each bridge was mobbed with traffic. Carts filled with fruit, buggies with all kinds of merchandise, rickshaws, and hundreds of people were all trying to go in opposite directions all at once. Frequently two large carts would block each other from crossing one of the narrow bridges, and the drivers would argue for twenty minutes about who should back all the way off. And everyone behind the loser of this debate would have to back off as well. This went on all day on each of the bridges.

Ollie, McGuffin, Dr. Broth, and Musashi had to wait an hour and a half before they could get on the first bridge. As they crossed, moving inch by inch, Ollie pointed out that the walls of the bridge were covered with posters. Each one challenged someone or some school to a fight or battle:

"Ryuji! Time for you to see your next life as a newt. Meet me at Gojo Avenue and try to defend yourself."

"Tsurukawa! You killed my mother-in-law, who, it's true, I never liked. But it's my duty to avenge her. Please meet me at Yoshida Hill on Tuesday. My apologies."

"Fusho school! You ignored our advice to stop fighting and take jobs as janitors. You think you can fight? Come prove it!"

"Quite a lot of avenging going on," said Ollie.

"Yes," said Musashi, "there used to be only two bridges here. But there was so much revenge going around that there wasn't enough room for all the posters—they had to build this bridge. It hasn't helped the traffic problem, though. The shogun says he'll put up the money for three more bridges if, once they're built, every bridge in Kyoto becomes one-way. And he insists that travel to any given place in the city require at most two bridge crossings. No one's sure if such demands can be met."

"But does the answer lie with the bridges?" asked Dr. Broth. "Perhaps we could just find some way to make each cellular automaton move at the same rate. Surely some sort of traffic regulator is a better solution."

Ollie looked to his right and left. He could see all the bridges from where he stood. "If he would free up the money for three new bridges," he said in a hypothetical tone, "and make every bridge one-way, traffic would move smoothly, and everyone would still be able to get to every part of town."

"Where would you put them?" asked Musashi.

"There's only one way to place them," said Ollie, "for the most efficient flow of traffic."

Brawny Bridge

THE BRIDGE CREAKED AND swayed from the weight of all the travelers. Dr. Broth held tightly to the railing as they inched along.

"Exactly how many tons can this bridge hold?" he asked.

"Tons? We measure such things in sumo wrestlers here. I believe this bridge is rated at five hundred wrestlers," said Musashi.

A pulse ran through the bridge.

"What's the people equivalent of a sumo wrestler?" asked Dr. Broth, nervously counting heads.

"Don't worry, these bridges are meant to sway a little. We're far from capacity."

"Just the same, I don't see why they didn't make the bridge bigger. Not only would it be sturdier and hold more people and rickshaws—sumo wrestlers, if you will—there would be plenty of room for more vengeance announcements. Instead of building three new bridges, they should build one that's three times as high, three times as long, and three times as wide. Then the bridge's capacity would be, let's see . . ."

A Hex Lesson

AFTER SLEEPING ON A mat on the floor of a blacksmith friend of Musashi's, and eating noodles for breakfast washed down with hot green tea, the trio decided that they'd best be on their way.

Musashi said that he regretted seeing them go but that he understood their endless search. "Forward, always forward," he said.

"Endless, yes," said Dr. Broth, "always forward? Perhaps not."

"Foreigners aren't safe traveling without a guide. I'd like to give you a few lessons before you continue on your journey," said Musashi.

Dr. Broth tried to explain that they'd be safe where they were going and wouldn't need to know how to wield a sword, but Ollie and McGuffin quickly interrupted him.

"We'd be honored," said Ollie.

"Do I get to carry a sword and cut my hair like that?" asked McGuffin.

"In the Samurai's path to perfection," said Musashi, "fashion follows dedication, my dedicated follower of fashion."

He led them to an empty lot and pulled out his sword.

"My technique is called the Way of the Two Swords, and two swords are used. But I think one will be enough for you to start with. Here's how it should be gripped." Musashi held the hilt with one hand just above the other. "Your grip is the foundation for everything else you do. If you have a weak grip, you'll have a weak stroke and all your movements will be unbalanced."

He handed the sword to Dr. Broth. As soon as Musashi let go, Dr. Broth's arms dropped to the ground with the weight of the steel.

"Maybe even this lesson is too advanced for us," said McGuffin.

"Well," Musashi said, somewhat disappointed, "I'll give you guys a wooden sword to take with you, and show you a few things you can practice after you've built up enough strength to, er, hold it properly. You can work up to these things on your own."

He demonstrated some exercises: slashing, thrusting, blocking, and "beating a hasty retreat," as Dr. Broth would say. "Possibly the most useful exercise in your case," Musashi remarked.

Pulling over a wooden cube from the side of the lot, Musashi pointed his sword at it. "Turning simple shapes into more complicated shapes is an excellent exercise once you've mastered the basic movements. It's a perfect way to unite mind and body in preparation for conflict. Out of this cube, for instance, I will create two two-dimensional hexagons with only one cut. I know you're not ready for the physical task of slicing it up—maybe you could use a block of tofu—but you ought to be able to figure out where I should make the cut."

"Yes, we do seem to be dividing things up an awful lot," said McGuffin.

Dr. Broth was checking the well-thumbed timetable bequeathed to him by his older self.

"I don't mean to cut the lesson short," he said, "but we should be leaving for Peru right about now."

Cornered

THE TRIO STOOD SURROUNDED by the heights of the Andes. Below them they could see the streets and buildings of a city laid out in the shape of a puma. A condor circled above them. And—no surprise to Dr. Broth and Ollie—there was no airport in sight.

"I don't feel so good," said Ollie, stumbling dizzily forward.

"That," said Dr. Broth, "is due to the altitude. The natives of the Andes have larger and stronger lungs so as to breathe more oxygen in the rarified air. The higher the altitude, the less air pressure, and, consequently, the brain gets less oxygen . . . *gasp* . . . hypoxia . . . and . . . *gasp.*" The doctor, turning blue, fell over wheezing for air.

"That's just like you lowlanders," said McGuffin, chuckling to himself. Holding his head in pain, Ollie sat down next to Dr. Broth.

Across the field in which they'd landed came a group of what seemed like several hundred men pulling an enormous stone with thick ropes. Their colorfully woven clothes were stained with sweat in the hot dry air.

"This oxygen deprivation is making me hallucinate," said Dr. Broth, "I'm seeing hundreds of men dragging a huge rock."

"Me too," said Ollie.

"What a coincidence," said McGuffin, "I'm neither sick nor hallucinating and I, too, see hundreds of men dragging a huge rock."

When the men had pulled the stone within a few feet of the foreigners, they stopped for a break. All the men began pulling leaves out of their pockets and filling their mouths.

The foreman studied the gaspers for a moment and then came over to them. "Strangers?" he asked.

Dr. Broth and Ollie nodded vigorously.

"I can tell," said the foreman, now examining McGuffin.

"We don't usually see alpacas with this color of wool."

Dr. Broth and Ollie nodded vigorously.

The Dizzying Heights of Peru

"Yep, I'd keep a close eye on this one. There's more than a few people that would like to get their hands on it. The Inca himself might like a cloak made of that wool. You may even be able to buy your way into being a Big Ear."

Dr. Broth and Ollie nodded vigorously.

"Are you all right? Seems like you haven't said a word since I showed up."

Dr. Broth and Ollie shook their heads vigorously.

"You're strangers from down there?" he asked, pointing over the nearest hill, "And you're feeling light-headed?"

More nodding from the underoxygenated pair.

"Here," said the foreman, handing them some leaves and little gray rocks. "Just chew those together, and you'll be feeling more clearheaded and energetic in no time. I should've thought of that right away."

They eagerly took the foreman's offerings. After a few minutes of mastication, the two were feeling lively again.

"Thank you, thank you. I thought I was going to die," said Ollie.

"Is there anything we can do to repay you?" asked Dr. Broth.

"You look like the intellectual type. Maybe you can help me with a small problem I've got." The foreman gave a signal to the crew and they picked up their ropes and started pulling again. The foreman led the pair down into the city below. They passed huge stone temples and walls until the foreman stopped in a little alley. Large stones of various sizes and shapes were scattered about.

"We're supposed to be building a wall here," said the foreman. "It's especially difficult with that twelve-cornered rock. We've already cut most of the stone and moved a lot of it here. But unfortunately the architect who'd planned everything was recently sacrificed to the sun. He died without telling me how to put these rocks together to make a wall."

"He didn't leave you any written instructions?" asked McGuffin.

"Well, you know, we haven't developed a written language."

"Not that it would do you any good," said Dr. Broth. "According to elementary transtopological mechanics, the polygonal interactions of the mesa fields creates a register that increases by the exponent of the vertices. With a twelve-cornered stone, this means the probability of success is one in five hundred and thirty thousand."

Ollie looked at all the stones. "Luck must be with us, then. I see a way these rocks can be put together, but they have to be assembled in the right order."

A Belt of Genius

"I'M AFRAID THAT PUTS me in debt to you. And a few coca leaves won't be enough to show my gratitude," said the foreman.

A crowd had started to form in the alley. The short, black-haired, big-lunged people were pointing in their direction and whispering among themselves.

"We probably seem very noble and statuesque to them," said Dr. Broth, "perhaps they think we're gods."

The crowd inched forward. *Oohs* and *aaahs* periodically leapt out of the whispering. "Maybe we should tell them," continued Dr. Broth to Ollie, "that though we do hope to spread our knowledge, to teach them the art and convenience of alphanumeric writing and the utility and efficiency of the wheel—that we are merely human, much like themselves."

At that moment, the crowd reached McGuffin. A dozen hands sank into his wool. Those closest bent over and rubbed the wool between their fingers.

"Nice fabric."

"What texture. What strong fibers."

"I can see this weaving up very well."

"Such rich colors."

"Have you ever seen anything like it, Murray?"

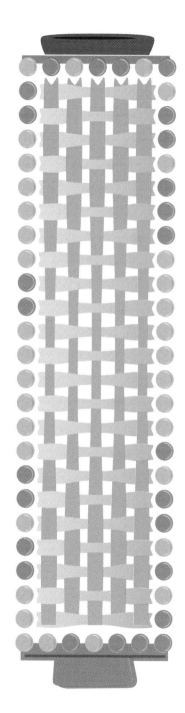

Some of them ran their hands across McGuffin's thick coat.

"I quite like this," the alpaca said.

"O.K., everybody, back off. Nothing to see here," said the foreman. "This alpaca belongs to these kind foreigners, and I'm sure they'd appreciate it if you'd respect their property just as you'd expect them to respect yours."

The crowd backed away despondently, but a few scruffy-looking individuals lingered at a distance for a last look at McGuffin.

"You've got some prize there," said the foreman. "Why don't you stay at my place tonight? My wife and I will make you an authentic Cuzco meal; you'll be safe, and you'll give me a chance to repay you for helping me with the wall."

So they tromped through the streets till they came to a small door in the side of a wall. Inside, the foreman's wife was making a belt of silver and gold medallions.

The foreman introduced his wife to his new friends, and then the couple set off to prepare the evening's meal.

Over the sumptuous spread of guinea pig, potatoes, and *chicha,* Ollie asked about the belt.

"That," said the foreman's wife, "is a belt I'm making for the Inca. I have eighty-two golden medallions and ninety-three silver medallions. But this belt has to be assembled according to the Inca's whim, and he wants every gold medallion to have an odd number of gold neighbors, diagonally as well as vertically and horizontally. I started with the border, but now I don't know how I'm going to finish it."

Ollie looked over at the belt.

"I could help you," he said.

"Please resist," said the foreman. "I can't afford to be even further in debt to you."

A Bend in the River

DR. BROTH EXPLAINED, OVER a few additional mugs of *chicha,* how the other Broth had lost his briefcase, leading to their travels all over the world.

"At the moment," he said, "I have no idea how to proceed, no idea what city to go to next, or even if it's worth it. By the time I get back to New York, someone else will be basking in the glory of my results."

"Don't take it so hard," said the foreman. "Tomorrow we'll go see one of the Inca's priests who'll tell you exactly what to do."

The foreman and his wife led them to their rooms and gave Dr. Broth and Ollie several alpaca wool blankets. To McGuffin they gave one of llama wool.

Dr. Broth woke up early the next morning, eager to see the priest about his luggage.

"Come on, let's go!" he shouted to everybody. "We've got to get there before the lines start."

Ollie reluctantly rolled out of bed and started climbing into his clothes while the doctor was pounding on the door of McGuffin's room.

"Come on, you lazy ruminant, time to wake up."

But there was no response.

"If you don't at least say something, I'm going to have to come in there and wake you up myself. I hope you're decent."

By now the foreman and his wife were up.

Impatient and irate, Dr. Broth threw the door open and marched in. McGuffin was nowhere to be seen.

"Where can he be?" asked Ollie.

"Look," said the foreman, pointing to the ground, "there's been a scuffle." Footprints of several pairs of feet marked the floor in a motley array around four streaks. "Alpaca rustlers."

Ollie and Dr. Broth followed the foreman as he traced the footsteps to the outside door. There the four streaks turned into hoofprints.

"Oh, no," sighed Ollie, "what do you think they've done with him?"

"Don't worry," said the foreman as they followed the footprints away from the house, "they'll certainly want him alive and unharmed. The dangerous part will be trying to get him back."

It quickly became clear that the tracks in the dirt were those of an alpaca and three men. After half an hour, they had followed the footprints to a river outside of town. The prints ended at the water's edge, by a V-shaped bend in the river.

"Do you think they rode him across?" asked Ollie.

"Not likely," said the foreman, "the water's too deep and rapid."

Nearby, two planks, each nine feet and three-quarters of an inch in length, sat in the mud.

"Those probably had something to do with it," said the foreman. "There's a few smudged footprints on them."

"But the planks aren't long enough to cross this ten-foot-wide river," said Dr. Broth.

"I think I know what they might have done," said Ollie, "and it looks like we'll have to do the same thing if we're going to follow them."

Con Cave Search

"WHY," ASKED OLLIE AS they trudged up a steep hill, "is everyone so keen on McGuffin's wool?"

"In general," answered the foreman, "alpaca wool is more valuable than that of the llama. It's softer and finer. But this McGuffin—his wool is like nothing we've ever seen. It's longer, and thicker, but still just as soft. Wool like that is fit for the Inca himself. Whoever's got a hold of him is bound to have great favor at court."

The tracks were becoming clearer as they ascended.

"I think we're gaining on them," said the foreman.

"Did they really think that climbing this hill was the best escape route? McGuffin's no mountain goat," puffed Dr. Broth.

"I've got a pretty good idea where they're going. On the top of this hill there's a boulder that covers a hole. The hole leads to a cave with a complex system of rooms. They don't call the place Rustlers' Haven for nothing."

They finally reached the top of the hill where the tracks led up to a solitary boulder and disappeared. The foreman directed Ollie and Dr. Broth to grab hold of a corner of the great rock and push. After a few dozen grunts and curses, the boulder rolled away. They jumped down into the hole. Dr. Broth turned on a flashlight.

"What's that?" asked the amazed foreman.

"This? It's just a penlight, er, a flashlight. Thomas Edison invented the light bulb and then with the advent of miniature batteries—"

"Point it over here."

On the wall was a chart with circles carved out at several intersections. Some of the circles were carved out entirely—making a dark concave indentation—while others were just the circumference of a circle.

"This is a map of all the rooms in this cave. We're here," said the foreman, pointing to a white star on the map. "All we've got to do is search every one of them. But

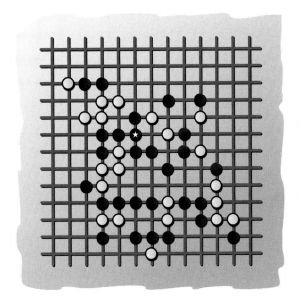

they're booby-trapped. We can only move one grid mark from a white circle and two—including turns—from a black one. Otherwise, the rooms will cave in on us—at least so a thief confessed to me under torture. Poor fellow. We need to find the rustlers as quickly as possible, though, or they are bound to go out for a lunch break."

Ollie examined the map for a few moments.

"There's one way that's more efficient than any other," he said, "and when we're done, we'll finish up right here."

Belted Again

THE FOREMAN, OLLIE, AND Dr. Broth trudged from room to room, with Dr. Broth's flashlight as their only source of illumination. After countless hours, they entered the second-to-last room.

"No alpacas in here," said the foreman for the umpteenth time.

"I guess we better learn how to haul rocks," said Dr. Broth to Ollie. "It doesn't look like we'll ever get out of the sixteenth century."

"Wait a second," said Ollie, "what's that sound?"

They put their ears up to the cave's wall. Next door, according to the map, was the last room. They could just make out the sounds of clinking and laughter.

"Listen," said Ollie, "sounds like someone's having a good time."

"You've got to be kidding me," came a deep voice through the wall before it was drowned out with chortles and guffaws. "He said that, did he? Har-har-har-har."

At Ease with the Ruffians

"And then," came a slightly higher-pitched voice, "he took us to this horrible restaurant. I couldn't be-lieve it!"

"That sounds like McGuffin," said Ollie. "What should we do?"

"Don't worry," said the foreman, "I'll take care of them with my *waraca.*" He pulled a slingshot from his belt and put three stones in it. Then he and the time travelers tiptoed to the entrance of the last room.

". . . so I looked right in his eye and sent a stream of spit at him," McGuffin was saying.

"Har-har—" One of the rustlers saw the foreman at the entrance. The room was silent other than the sound of McGuffin chewing his cud. The rustlers stood up all at once, reaching into their belts. The fore-man let fly with his *waraca,* and each of the three stones found a forehead. The thieves fell to the ground unconscious.

"Let's go!" shouted Ollie.

"Hey . . . I was having a good time," said McGuffin as he followed them out reluctantly.

On the way home, the foreman explained that they should make a coat from McGuffin's wool and give it to the Inca as soon as possible. Once the Inca had such a gift and knew its source, no one would dare steal McGuffin.

"Until then," said the foreman, "I'll keep my *waraca* loaded."

That night the foreman's wife showed everyone what they had to do to make a magnificent *kumpi* coat for the Inca. Ollie sheared McGuffin, Dr. Broth spun the thread, the foreman's wife worked the loom, and the foreman assembled the coat.

"Ow! Careful back there," said McGuffin as Ollie hurried to take the wool. "This is what I left my good time–loving companions for?"

McGuffin soon grew too tired to complain and fell asleep as the others worked through the night. In the morning they took the elaborate coat of his wool and the belt that Ollie had helped the foreman's wife assemble to the Inca's temple. They were first in line to make an offering.

The foreman's wife meekly approached the bat-skin-and-gold-clad Inca.

"Here is the belt I promised you," she said, "but to show our ever-growing love and obedience, we have also brought you this coat made from the wool of a unique animal."

The Inca took the gifts and ran his hands over the cloth.

"You have outdone yourselves. You may have anything you wish—within reason."

"Master, our friends, who brought us the extraordinary alpaca, wish to return to their home and would like to meet with the high priest for his advice."

"Whatever you want," said the Inca mechanically, enraptured with his gifts. "This coat is so magnificent that I would like you to make me yet another belt, even more intricate and splendid than this one you've given me."

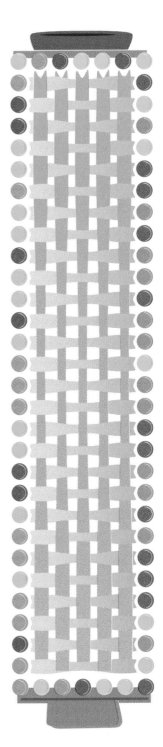

"We're at your service," said the foreman's wife.

"This time," continued the Inca, "I want seventy yellow medallions, seventy-four orange medallions, and sixty-six red medallions. Place them on the belt so that every yellow medallion has an odd number of yellow neighbors and every orange medallion has an even number of orange neighbors, including diagonals. The border has already been laid out for you. By tomorrow, please."

"Particular, isn't he?" muttered McGuffin.

The foreman's wife hurried out to get a start on the complicated belt.

"What am I going to do?" she cried, stumped after finishing two rows. Then she remembered that Ollie was there to help her.

The Priest of Forethought

THAT EVENING THE FOREMAN led the trio to the great Coricancha: the temple of the sun. In the center of the temple was a throne of pure gold on an altar of pure gold on a floor of pure gold. On the throne was a man, seemingly of flesh, though without a doubt large portions of him were gold as well. His chest was plated with gold, his earlobes were plugged with gold, and his head was crowned with a fan of gold like a peacock's tail.

"Oh, highest of men, descendent of the sun, the Inca has given us permission to ask of you a small request," said the foreman who, as he knelt, was trying to pull the others down as well.

"So I have been informed," said the priest. "Why must you come to me?"

"Because you are the mouthpiece of the sun, who, despite the immensity of his power, cannot speak himself."

"Well said. That's the sun's opinion, anyway. What is it you actually want?"

The foreman had succeeded in pulling McGuffin onto his side.

"These friends of mine," he said, "have come from another time and another place. They are looking for some kind of sacred papers, which they know exist somewhere in their own time, but they don't know where. They hope to return to this time of theirs soon and thought that you, with your powers, could tell them where they should go."

The priest mused on this for a while.

"That's no easy feat!" he said. "There are many different times in many different worlds. The possibilities of each moment branch into new worlds and times, each of which has its own possibilities, which branch into new worlds and new times and so on and so on. In order to determine where they should go I must first determine where they've come from out of an infinite number of possibilities. Then, having understood such a thing, if I should be so lucky, I must peer into this time, so foreign from our own, and determine where this certain mash of dead plant is existing. Yet another infinity of possibilities!"

"I'm sorry, forgive me . . . ," said the foreman.

"But it can be done!" the priest interrupted, "provided we have the right animal."

The priest descended from his throne and approached McGuffin, who, while lying on his side, had dozed off during the sermon. The priest reached down and put his hand in McGuffin's clipped wool.

"This," spoke the priest firmly, "is exactly what we're looking for. Isn't this the Inca's favorite new alpaca?"

"Yes, it is," said the foreman.

"And you say the Inca knows about this? That he sent you here?"

The foreman nodded.

"Then I think I can help you," said the priest.

He pulled McGuffin up by his chin and led him to the altar.

"It's very simple," continued the priest. "The greater the offering, the more accurate the prediction. And what could be a greater sacrifice than this extraordinary animal—the Inca's favorite. I'll just slit his throat and watch how he falls. That'll tell us most of what we need to know. And a quick look at the insides of his lungs before he dies will give us the particulars."

The priest drew a great knife from his robes. McGuffin began to bleat.

"Ummm, excuse me," said Ollie as politely as possible, "but we'll need him."

"What's that?" asked the priest, already looking for the vein on McGuffin's neck.

"He's our only way of getting back. If you kill him, you may be able to tell us where to go, but we won't be able to get there."

"You need him? Are you sure?"

"Quite."

"Well, that's too bad. I was rather looking forward to sacrificing the beast."

"Beast? *I'm* not the knife-wielding psychopath," said McGuffin.

"There's no other way you can help us?" asked Ollie.

"Without a sacrifice?"

"If it's possible."

"Well, yes. I suppose there is another way," said the priest, "but it's not nearly as accurate. Could be off by a few hundred miles."

He went back to the throne, mucked around underneath it, and came back with a bat-skin bag. "What was it you were looking for?"

"A brown attaché case," chimed in Dr. Broth. "Buckles on the side . . . with my life's work, about half a foot wide—"

The priest waved his hands over the bag, chanted, and looked toward where the sun had just set. Then he spilled the contents of the bag on the floor.

"When we put those pieces together, we'll have a symbol representing a major commercial power from your time. You should head there."

"Well, Ollie, I guess I may as well let you try it," conceded Dr. Broth.

"I'm sorry," said Ollie, "I'm a little shaken up after seeing that knife so close to McGuffin's throat. I can't think straight."

Dr. Broth and the foreman struggled to put the pieces together.

Wrangle in Time

DR. BROTH, OLLIE, AND a shorn McGuffin were flying through the ether when the doctor started grumbling.

"It seems to me that we haven't once gone to the place where we've meant to, and I think I know why," he said.

"You do, do you. Well don't keep it to yourself, genius," said the alpaca.

"I've noticed," continued the doctor, ignoring McGuffin's comment, "that we seem to be hopping from one place to another fairly quickly. At the rate we're going, we're proba-bly approaching the speed of light, where Hyde's time-dilution effect comes into play."

"I don't know much about that," said Ollie, "I think alpacas have their own methods. Maybe this time-dilution effect could explain why his wool grows back so quickly when we travel."

"It's simple though. At this speed, we're traveling through time at a different rate than the people still on Earth. If I can just work that into the formula, I think I can get us to Charles de Gaulle Airport just as the bag arrives." The doctor rolled his eyes to the tops of their sockets, counted a few numbers finger by finger, and looked at his watch. "If we descend now, by my calculation, we ought to be there right on time."

"Whatever you say," remarked McGuffin with a stubbly shrug. In an instant they were floating high above the ocean, not a clod of land in sight.

"Doesn't look much like Paris to me."

Far beneath them a ship was cutting through the water and filling the air with steam.

"I think we better stick with my methods," added McGuffin, preparing to jump back into the ionosphere.

"Wait," cried Ollie, "I think they're trying to tell us something."

Some people on the steamer's deck were waving six big banners at them.

"You're right," said Dr. Broth, "it looks to me like a slight derivation of the classic

Remorse Code, the same one used by the Ottomans in the war against Transylvania. Each group of black circles represents a word or letter, though different letters *could* be represented by different groupings in alternate clusters for the sake of secrecy. In this case it looks like—"

"Actually," interrupted Ollie, "it looks to me as if they've made a mistake. If they would just rearrange the cards, I think you'd know right away what they're trying to say."

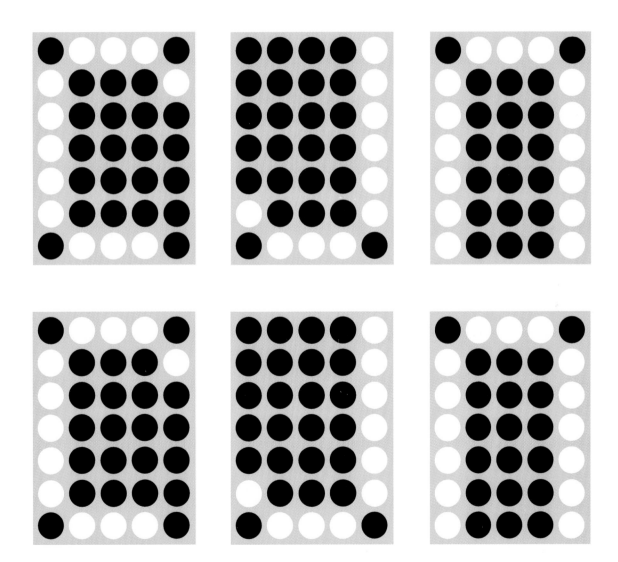

What Mortals These Fools Be

AS THE TRIO TOUCHED down on the boat's deck, a small crowd, bouncing up and down and peering over one another's shoulders nervously, gathered around them. Many of them had yo-yos; some wore multicolored propeller caps; and nearly all of them had fingers in their mouth and drool on their chins. At length, a bearded man in a cone-shaped hat—a wizard's hat, or perhaps a dunce cap—pulled himself out of the crowd.

"Ah, thank you, thank you very kindly for coming to our assistance. You're most welcome, most grateful, et cetera, et cetera. Please make yourselves at home. Is there anything I can do for you?"

"Perhaps you could tell us where we are?" inquired the doctor. "By my calculations we should be somewhere within the Paris metropolitan conurbation. If this beast had descended when I'd instructed—"

"Ha, ha. That's funny. I may be stupid, but I *can* tell you that we're far from France. You see, you're on board the SS *Dimvit,* a seagoing vessel for the discriminating imbecile." The wizard put an arm around Dr. Broth. "For years, village idiots have worked long, hard hours for little or no pay, with no vacation and no appreciation. We, some of us, finally realized that without pooling our resources—few as they are— without solidarity, we would never make a step forward. So we joined forces, built this . . . idiotic . . . ship, and decided to circle the globe, giving village idiots and the quieter suburban eccentrics as well as volatile inner-city loonies an opportunity to see the world. These fools would never have a chance to see beyond the next yurt, well-kept lawn, or abandoned building otherwise. Right now we've just left Bermuda for Florida. Would you like to see the bar, the convention center, the poolroom? This is a pleasure craft, you know. 'Pleasant and stupid'—that's our motto."

The flustered Dr. Broth extracted himself from the wizard's embrace. He felt ready to retire to the bar.

"Excuse me," inquired Ollie, "but is there, perhaps some problem? We saw your sign and thought maybe we could help."

A gurgle and a burp from below interrupted them for a moment.

"How could I forget!" the wizard smacked his forehead. "Yes, we are, in fact, in the midst of a terrible disaster. Our ship is sinking, and no one knows how to fix it."

"I bet our infallible professor will have a few ideas," said McGuffin.

"I did, in fact, work on some body-displacement theory in my youth, and have spent—"

Another gurgle and groan from below drowned out the doctor's words.

Landing among the Stupids

"I'm afraid we don't have time for that," said the wizard, tugging on Broth's sleeve, "follow me."

They marched to the bow of the ship, descended a spiral staircase, and entered the hull. Idiotic faces stared at them from above.

On the starboard side, water was rushing into the ship through a large star-shaped hole. On the floor, sloshing back and forth in a foot of water, lay a similarly large four-legged starfish.

"You see? That sucker, fleeing from some shark probably, lost a leg and punched his way in here. All we have to fix it is this six-foot-by-six-foot piece of Styrofoam."

"Styrofoam?" asked the alpaca.

"Sure. Our hull's made out of Styrofoam. All those other boat-building idiots don't realize that Styrofoam floats better than iron. But this is the only extra piece we've got."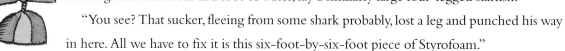

"I don't see that that ought to be a problem," said Dr. Broth. "The process for recycling Styrofoam requires only a handful of chemicals—easily acquired. We'll make a cast of the starfish and pour a few liters of polystyrene—"

"Oh, I don't think all that's necessary," said Ollie. "I can cut the square into nine pieces to fit the hole—with some glue, of course."

Kettle Power

OVERJOYED AT THE SIGHT of the mended hull, the wizard slapped Ollie on the back and invited everyone to the bar for ice cream and sardines.

"What's that whistling sound?" asked Ollie as they stepped onto the staircase.

"Whistling sound? What whistling sound?" asked the wizard.

"That high-pitched whistling sound. You don't hear it?"

The wizard paced for a minute, pulling on his chin.

"Ooooooh. You mean that incredibly annoying, mind-numbing screech? That's our boiler room. It powers the ship. Would you like to see it?"

"Certainly," said Ollie, after cautious glances from the others. The wizard led them toward the stern. Puffs of steam spilled around the edges of a rusty iron door. Putting his fingers in his ears, the wizard pushed open the door with his elbow and stepped inside. The others followed with their fingers in their ears as well.

Two idiots were hurriedly running around the room—a fairly large one—filling about a hundred black iron stoves with coal. On top of each stove were four teakettles, boiling away. A third idiot ran from burner to burner, filling any kettles that had boiled dry.

Dr. Broth stepped back, filled with awe and wonder.

"That," he said emphatically, "is a remarkable feat of engineering!"

"If someone's got an extra finger or two, could you stick them in my ears?" said the alpaca.

"Myshkin!" shouted the wizard over his shoulder. Immediately an idiot appeared, jumped onto McGuffin's back and put his fingers into the animal's ears.

"Much better, thank you," said the alpaca, "they should hand out these idiots at rock concerts."

After the steam display, the wizard and the time travelers headed upstairs to the bar. As they sat musing glumly over their ice cream and sardines, McGuffin noticed a strange table nearby: an octagon with a square hole in the center.

"What's that for?" he asked.

"That," replied the wizard, "is our pool table. You see, we idiots have a hard time with all the angles involved in a typical pool game. So we developed our own table to make it a little easier. One pocket. Otherwise the same rules: Whoever sinks the first ball chooses solids or stripes. If you scratch while going for the eight ball, you lose, et cetera, et cetera. Have to call your shots. I'd ask you for a game, but I'm afraid some idiot's ripped off all the felt to make miniature Christmas trees for his dollhouse."

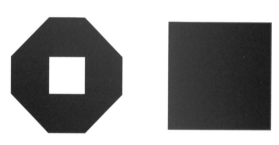

"That's really too bad," said Dr. Broth. "I enjoy applying a bit of multivariant geometry to modified rules."

"You don't happen to have any extra felt lying around, do you?" asked Ollie.

"We do, but unfortunately it's in the shape of a plain old square."

"If the square's sides are the same distance apart as the table's, then I think I can make it fit with just a few folds and one cut."

I Want Some Seafood, Mama

"SHALL WE RETIRE TO the dinning room?" asked the wizard, after they'd played a few rounds of one-holed pool.

"You mean the dining room, of course," said Dr. Broth.

"Dinning room," said the wizard with a condescending glance at the doctor. "The waiters and the cooks make such a din with all the plates and glasses they smash—well, dinning makes sense to us."

The wizard led them to a great hexagonal room filled with hexagonal tables. No one else was there. They sat down at a table near the door. A crash came from the kitchen. "It's best we sit as far from the kitchen as possible. The noise can be deafening."

Their hexagonal table was made up of thirty-six smaller hexagons with a hexagonal hole in the center.

"Oh, no," cried McGuffin, "you're not going to make us play Variable Nebulaese Checkers, are you?"

The wizard looked at him strangely.

"Obviously not," said Dr. Broth, "there's a hole in the center. What's on the menu?"

"Seafood, of course," said the wizard, "that's what the hole is for: all the shells."

The steel doors to the kitchen swung open and a waiter emerged carrying some glasses and a pitcher of water. On his way across the room, several of the glasses slid off his tray and shattered on the floor.

"I knew that was going to happen!" he shouted to them. "Don't worry, I've got extras."

At their table he filled a few glasses for everyone and asked what they wanted to eat.

"We'll have the seafood," said the wizard.

"Right," said the waiter, and he scurried away to the kitchen.

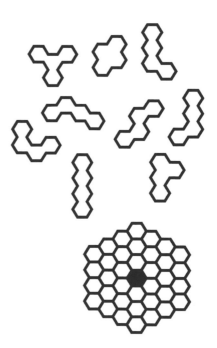

Half an hour and several explosions later, the waiter returned with a tray the size of a surfboard filled with ten oddly shaped platters. Three-quarters of the way across the room one of the platters hurled itself to the floor with a mighty crash.

"I knew that was going to happen!" said the waiter. "Don't worry, I've got extras."

"It's a good thing you dropped that other dish," said Dr. Broth when the waiter arrived at the table. "I don't see how we're going to fit all that on the table."

"Actually," said Ollie, examining the oddly shaped stainless-steel plates, "there's only one way we can fit the remaining platters on the table and still leave the hole clear for the shells."

Urchin Aversion

FOLLOWING OLLIE'S INSTRUCTIONS, THE waiter arranged the steel platters of seafood on the table. There were oysters, clams, mussels, lobsters, crabs, conch, scallops, eel, and sea urchins. The four of them attacked the food, tearing apart claws, swallowing oysters in a single gulp, and throwing the hard parts into the center hole. As they ate, the waiter returned again and again with seconds, thirds, and fourths. The discarded shells filled the center hole, and the waiter began laying platters across that hexagon as well. They'd finished everything several times over. Everything, that is, but the sea urchins and eel.

"Thank goodness they don't just serve ice cream and sardines. I'm ready for fifths, personally," said McGuffin, "but I'd rather not have any more urchins or eel."

"I, too, pass on the urchins and eel," said Ollie.

"I don't even want to see any more urchins or eel," said Dr. Broth. "Vile creatures."

"The eel comes on a Y-shaped platter and the sea urchin on the doubled-up squarish platter. My advice to you," said the wizard, handing them a stack of seven hexagonal napkins, "is to wait until he's cleared the table, then place these seven napkins so that no sea urchin or eel platters will even fit on the table."

"Won't he just move the napkins?" asked Dr. Broth.

"You forget," said the wizard, "we're dealing with an idiot."

THEY COULD HEAR THE waiter crashing around in the kitchen, preparing the sixth serving as they finished the fifth.

"I can't eat another bite," said Ollie.

Dr. Broth and McGuffin, visibly bloated, nodded in agreement.

"I'm afraid there's no stopping that idiot once he's started," said the wizard.

"Can't we do something with the napkins?" asked Ollie.

"Sure," said the wizard, "but I don't have enough napkins to cover the whole table."

"That's no problem," said Ollie, "we don't even need to cover half the table with napkins. If they're placed right, the waiter won't be able to place a single platter on the table."

"We better start," said Dr. Broth. "Here comes the idiot now." A crash resounded in the room.

"I knew that was going to happen," called out the waiter. "Don't worry, I've got extras."

Cacophonous Comestibles

Some Gaulle

"DON'T YOU THINK IT'S time we tried to make our way to Charles de Gaulle?" asked Dr. Broth as they left the dinning room.

"You're not leaving already, are you?!" exclaimed the wizard, grabbing Dr. Broth by the shoulder. "I was hoping to make you an honorary idiot."

The trio stepped on the deck and said their teary good-byes. The idiots gazed at the heavens, their beanies twirling in the salted breeze.

Ollie, McGuffin, and Dr. Broth soon appeared outside of Paris. Perhaps unsurprisingly, there was no airport to be seen. Instead, they were surrounded by a group of foul-smelling drunkards in red caps and yellow trousers. Several prisoners sat with their hands tied behind their backs in a horse-drawn cart. A cry went up amongst the crowd.

"Spies!"

One particularly disheveled-looking man approached the doctor with a knife.

"You wouldn't happen to know where the nearest airport is?" asked the doctor.

"Spies!" shouted the man. "Into the cart!"

Keeping as close together as possible, Ollie, McGuffin, and the doctor were herded onto the cart with the other bound prisoners.

"Welcome to our bogus wagon, dudes," said one of the captives.

"Hey, Ollie," whispered McGuffin, "those two prisoners look familiar."

Ollie squinted. "You're right. It's Bill and Ted from the movie."

McGuffin pointed to the corner. "And isn't that the two-thousand-year-old man?"

The older man shook his head and turned to the others: "More characters from some time-travel shtick. Tell me if I'm wrong."

"As a matter of fact, you're right," said Dr. Broth. "Could you please explain this distressing situation?"

"Sure, sure," said the old man, "these jokers in the red yarmulkes are rounding up any antidisestablishmentarians they can get their hands on. Or maybe it's the disestablishmentarians they're after, I can't remember."

Carted Away

"Which are you?" asked McGuffin.

"Me? I'm just an actor," said the man, "but you make one nutty history flick and you get stuck in the French Revolution. 'It's good to be the king,' my butt!"

"I guess that explains why we're here," said McGuffin.

"All kinds of time travelers are trapped here," continued the man. "Over there is Kevin from *Time Bandits.* I loved that movie."

"Thanks, Mel," said the little boy.

"And I was an extra in *Quantum Leap,*" said another man, "but my buddy here was Phineas Bogg on *Voyagers!*"

"Me, I had just one line on an old *Star Trek* episode," said a nondescript man in a blue velour shirt. "You know, the one with Joan Collins as guest star?"

"But where are they taking us, and why?" asked Ollie.

"Looks like we're going to lose our heads," said Mel. "When the revolutionary types heard what kinda dough we rake in, they chalked us up as aristocrats."

They sat disconsolately as the wagon rattled down the country road.

"You know, before I die, there's one thing I'd like to do," mumbled Bill through his gag.

"Oh yeah? What's that? Catch a perfect wave or just some kinda wild party?" asked Ted.

"No. I've been trying to solve this hellacious cryptic crossword for years. I wanted to do it myself, but now that I'm gonna totally die, I'd just like to know what the answers are."

"What's a cryptic crossword?" asked McGuffin.

Ollie explained how each clue in a cryptic crossword has two parts. One side is the definition and the other wordplay. The hard part is finding out which is which. Wordplay can include anagrams, hidden words, and other instructions found within the clue.

"Where is it?" asked Ollie eagerly.

"You'll have to fish it out of my back pocket," said Bill, with a glance at his manacled wrists.

ACROSS

1. Fish begat strange cloth luggage (9)
6. A Page hid insect (5)
9. Short record in Dept. of Transportation stockpile (5)
10. Ride explodes NASA trout (9)
11. Drunken singin' about northern portions of American pastime (7)
12. Car tore about Chernobyl (7)
13. Zero dessert for sitcom kid (4)
15. Unsettling change, or a place for settling down? (9)
18. Weird? Yes. Newark is where the solution is found. (6, 3)

20. Race car in dynamic section (4)
22. Without university, a guess about the French is eternal. (7)
24. Test Merlin without ER demon. (7)
26. Oboes in steamship, oddly, become craze. (9)
27. The seven nuisances embrace boredom. (5)
28. A light streak on fabric (5)
29. Ring after noticing strange disguise (9)

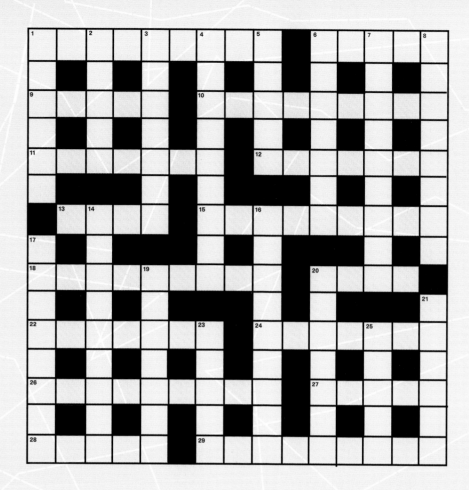

DOWN

1. CD idea spun for club attendant (6)
2. To tear up directions is mature? (5)
3. Understanding English, wild teen grasps New Testament. (7)
4. Jack's passage began without grand small talk. (9)
5. Gun or reptile? (5)
6. From havoc, Adonis, comes strange fruit. (7)
7. A country's interior has most of Earth left in hand. (9)
8. Discouraged, Koppel turned up and screwed up. (8)
14. "Pressure Serbs," say hairy pedestrians. (9)
16. Nice orgy falls apart after first college of cold science. (9)
17. Rain around a sheep lover (8)
19. Mere eccentric son is essayist. (7)
20. Part icky strange brew, initial Guinness is *Titanic* sinker. (7)
21. Color in one surrounded by stormy god (6)
23. Gibson's novels scintillate somewhat if read in reverse. (5)
25. Law agent shot in a veranda (5)

Conquer and Divide

THE CART WITH OUR heroic trio and their fellow time-traveling stars continued its melancholy journey over the potholed road to Paris. All those great minds focused on the cryptic crossword, perhaps in an attempt to block out the crowd of drunken peasants traveling with the cart on all sides. They were working on four down.

" 'Grand small talk?' What's that?" asked Ted.

"That's an oxymoron," said Dr. Broth.

"And that," said Mel nodding toward a peasant woman in a short skirt, "is one foxy moron. If they've got to be stupid, might as well make 'em foxy. That's what Uncle Sal used to say, anyway."

The cart stopped suddenly, sending its unwilling passengers hurtling forward. Bill's pencil flew out and landed in a clod of dirt.

"The marquis Mark's chateau!" went up a cry. At once the crowd of peasants ran at the fortress off the road and began axing the door and smashing windows.

"They're gonna strip ole Marquis Mark of everything but his underwear," said Mel.

Mere minutes later, the crowd hurried back to the cart as best they could, each peasant now carrying as much loot as possible. Most of them reassembled around the cart and began inspecting their booty.

A loud thud followed by a series of curses came from the chateau door. A group of thirteen peasants were struggling to get a huge square painting outside. The task would have been difficult enough, without the insults, and the tugging and pulling.

After several more bangs and foulmouthed remarks, they emerged carrying the enormous portrait of the marquis himself riding a pony in his underwear. He *and* the pony, in fact, were wearing underwear. Matching underwear. A Watteau original. When they'd brought the masterpiece up to the cart, they started arguing over how to divvy up the painting among them. They knew enough to know that a

Watteau was of considerable value, so they each wanted to be sure to have an equal section of the painting. The frame, however, was made of gold—a material whose value was easier to comprehend and easier to exchange—so the thirteen peasants also wanted to be sure to get an equal section of it as well.

Everyone had their knives in hand, ready to cut out their portion, but they could reach no consensus as to how to proceed.

"I can tell you how to divide up that square," said Ollie, "so that each of you gets an equal section of the painting and the frame."

"Don't help them!" hissed Dr. Broth. "That's a Watteau. It must be of historical importance."

"It is a Watteau," put in Mel, "but it's a Watteau of Marquis Mark in his underwear."

Captivity, Inequality, Misanthropy

AS SOON AS THE THIRTEEN peasants had their frame fraction and picture portion hidden away in their sacks, two groups broke out into a yelling match. A family of craftsmen and a family of farmers both felt that the marquis's land should be theirs. The craftsmen argued that they should have the land because they needed the lumber for wood and fire—the farmers could farm any type of land. The farming family, on the other hand, pointed out that the craftsmen could do their work in a much smaller area and didn't need acre upon acre of the marquis's land. The craftsmen admitted that they didn't need the entire estate, but the farmers were reluctant to let them choose which part of it they wanted. It soon became clear that the marquis's estate had one of the best playgrounds in the country, which all the peasants coveted, and that this was what the two factions really wanted. After much wrangling, the craftsmen stormed off in a huff. "Divide the land however you like," they said as they left, "just be sure that we get half the playground. And no cheating with wavy lines. One straight division."

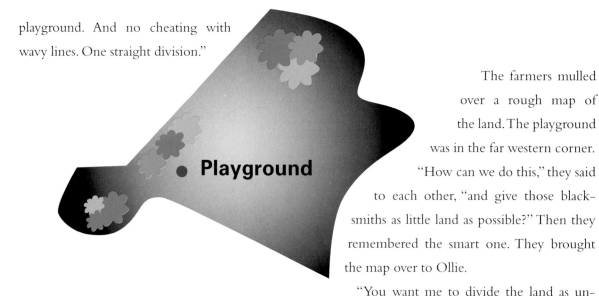

Playground

The farmers mulled over a rough map of the land. The playground was in the far western corner. "How can we do this," they said to each other, "and give those blacksmiths as little land as possible?" Then they remembered the smart one. They brought the map over to Ollie.

"You want me to divide the land as unequally as possible with a single line that passes through the playground—is that right?"

They said it was. After a quick perusal, Ollie drew the slash for them.

Head Choppers and Code Breakers

DESPITE OLLIE'S HELPFUL SUGGESTIONS for how to divide up their booty, the peasants' sympathy toward him did not increase. They chucked him back in the cart and hauled the crew toward Paris. Early the next morning, the anxiety of the captives acquired form as the cart pulled into the Place de la Révolution. On a platform, in the middle of a rowdy crowd, towered the ominous frame of the guillotine.

Dr. Broth was strangely calm.

"It's quite a good thing we arrived after they instituted the guillotine as the method of decapitation. I wouldn't want to be axed."

"Do you mean to say that you're resigned to having your head lopped off?" asked Mel.

"Is that what these dudes are going to do to us?" asked Bill.

"I merely mean to point out," said Dr. Broth, "that the guillotine is a humane and efficient form of execution."

"Still lops your head off," Mel noted.

The cart careened to a halt, throwing the bruised passengers against one another. Rough hands pulled them out and threw them into a line at the base of the platform. Dr. Broth, Ollie, and McGuffin stood at the front.

"I don't suppose there's any way we can get out of this," said Ollie.

"Not unless you can prove you're as poor as a muskrat and your blood isn't older than the milk you had for breakfast," said Mel.

"The only Bourbon in my blood came from a shot glass," said McGuffin.

"Maybe we can offer the executioner something," said Bill. "How 'bout our shoes?"

"I think he gets them even if you don't offer," said Mel.

Suddenly Mel nudged Dr. Broth in the ribs and handed him a piece of paper. "This just came from down the line,"

20021	00202	11200	01101	00102
10022	00102	20100	11100	01102
10121	00102	20011	11101	01111
21111	01212	20112	11112	00111
12111	11211	20201	11222	10012
01211	10201	21101	02222	20112
10111	10201	11102	01211	10201
21011	10110	00202	00101	10110
11002	00121	00102	01002	11120

he whispered. "Seems to be some kind of code. You don't happen to know it, do you?"

Dr. Broth stared intently at nine rows of five numbers, each five digits in length. "Looks like some variation of binary code, perhaps a trinary code, but, ah, no, I'm not familiar with this particular one."

"Oh, may I have a go at it? It may look like forty-five letters but it's really fifty," said Ollie cheerfully. "There's a binary code embedded in the trinary, but you have to read between the lines." After a few moments, he whispered a few words into McGuffin's ear.

A Mesmerizing Performance

WHEN THE CROWD'S SHOUTS for blood reached a deafening level, the executioner summoned McGuffin up on the platform. McGuffin, wobbling with fear, climbed the stairs and headed toward the guillotine. The executioner invited him to stick his head on the wooden rest beneath the blade. Instead, McGuffin mumbled the few words that Ollie had told him to say. The executioner went pale and staggered backward.

When he had composed himself, he approached the edge of the platform and addressed the crowd.

"Ladies and Gentlemen, please be kind enough to excuse a short delay. The blade has not yet been sharpened. It will take just a few moments for me to replace it with a finely ground one for your better amusement. Thank you." He then untied the rope and let it fall.

"Firing blanks," said Mel.

The executioner replaced the old blade with a new one of uneven color. After he'd hauled it back to the top, he repeated his request for McGuffin to put his head in the guillotine's neck rest.

"I thought we had an understanding," said McGuffin.

"Don't worry," whispered the executioner, "just stick your head in there for show."

McGuffin, not having much choice in the matter, placed his head on the rest. The executioner cut the rope and the blade fell.

"Ow," said McGuffin, his head now framed by shiny metal.

At first the crowd was stunned. The sight of McGuffin's head in front of the blade but still alive, sent a hush over the mob. But soon a rogue noticed the wooden half moon at the edge of the stage. This had been inserted into a notch in the blade and had popped out upon colliding with McGuffin's neck. They began to yell foul play.

"We want blood!"

"No exceptions! Roll the beast's head!"

Inspired by the agitators, the whole bloodthirsty throng screamed for vengeance. At any moment, it seemed, the crowd would storm the platform and tear apart McGuffin and the executioner.

Meanwhile, an intense bearded spectator stood a few feet from Ollie and Dr. Broth, taking notes on the unfolding events.

"It's Dr. Mesmer, inventor of hypnotism," said Dr. Broth to Ollie. "Maybe he can help us."

"Excuse me," said Dr. Broth to Mesmer, "I assume you are taking notes to let the world know of this atrocity. Perhaps you can help us."

"Actually, I'm just keeping track of the cruelty, inefficiency, and overall shoddiness of that ridiculous machine," said Mesmer. "Dr. Guillotine dares to say that my theory of animal magnetism is bunk, while he offers the world this ineffectual head chopper."

"If you really want to get back at him," suggested Ollie, "you could help us get our friend out of there alive. It wouldn't make Dr. Guillotine's machine look too good. And our friend does happen to be innocent. But you better hurry, it's only a matter of seconds before they attack him."

Mesmer mulled over the possibility for a second.

"I could try to hypnotize the crowd, but unfortunately I don't have the tools."

"If only my phaser weren't made of wood," said the *Star Trek* extra.

"What is it you need?" Dr. Broth asked Mesmer.

"Just a spiral to twirl in front of them. Works every time."

"Why don't you use that?" asked Ollie, pointing to a box on Dr. Mesmer's belt labeled Portable Instant Hypnokit.

"Well, it came from the factory unassembled, and they didn't include the instructions."

Ollie looked over the kit. It had forty-eight squares; half of them were white and half were black. In a few seconds Ollie had arranged them into a spiral and fixed them together with some "*fou* glue" included with the kit.

Dr. Mesmer Calms the Crowd

Mesmer hurried onto the platform and began spinning the spiral in front of the crowd.

"You're getting very sleepy!" he shouted at them, barely audible through the din of vengeful whooping. "Your eyelids are getting heavier and heavier."

To the astonishment of Ollie and Dr. Broth, who wisely kept their eyes on McGuffin instead of the spiral, the crowd became suddenly quiet. Mesmer convinced them that they were chickens named Glub and that they were holding a baby. Then he told them that the baby had just urinated on them and that they should take off their clothes and go home. Which they did.

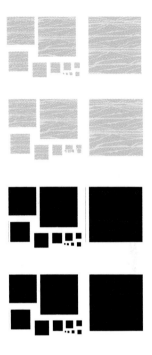

A Wild Suggestion

DR. MESMER, DR. BROTH, Ollie, and especially McGuffin ran terrified from the square while the crowd stumbled home. They hurried to the nearest place they could think of. Being tourists, every one of them, they headed into Notre Dame. After McGuffin's narrow escape, the high arches, colored light, and sense of peace overwhelmed them. They reverently took a seat in a rear pew.

"Amazing," said Dr. Broth.

"Mesmerizing," said Dr. Mesmer, "I could use this place to develop my ideas."

"A perfect place to further your invention of subconscious suggestive susceptibility," said Dr. Broth.

"Yes, you're right. If you'd like, I'll demonstrate on the alpaca."

"Well, I haven't lost my keys or anything, but maybe you could tell me who I was in a past life," said McGuffin.

"Easily done," said Mesmer, spinning the spiral Ollie had assembled for him. "You are getting veeeery sleepy."

"I am?" said McGuffin.

"Verrrry, verry sleeeepy. Now imagine you are descending a staircase into a pitch-black cellar; you can barely see the steps in front of you. . . ."

"Listen pal, I almost had my head lopped off a few seconds ago. Save the spooky stuff for the chickens."

Dr. Mesmer turned to Dr. Broth and shrugged.

"The patient must be willing, of course."

"Do you claim that the chickens you've hypnotized were willing?"

"Most definitely."

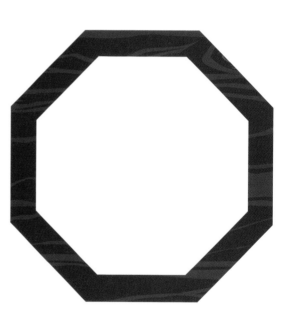

"And that mob back there?" asked McGuffin.

"Pacifists at heart."

Just then some workmen passed their pew, pushing a ten-foot octagon.

"You say they want us to cut this thing into sixty-four identical sections?" asked one of the workmen to the other.

"That's right. Something about scenes of the sixty-four martyrs of the Revolution that bit it last Tuesday. I don't know how we're going to do it."

"Here's another chance to find out how willing a hypnotee has to be," said Ollie. He spun the spiral at the workmen. As soon as they glanced at it they froze. Ollie had to jump up to save the octagon from toppling. Then he whispered a few words into the first workman's ear, sat back down, and clapped his hands. The workmen snapped awake and continued as if they'd never stopped.

"Oh, it's as easy as *tourte,*" said the first workman.

An Unexpected Turn

AS THE WORKMEN FINISHED dividing the octagon, the tranquility of the church was shattered by the sound of a flock of clucking peasants walking by.

"Ah, yes," said Dr. Mesmer with a sigh, "I suppose it's my duty, having taken the hypnocratic oath, to snap those hairy chickens out of their trance and return them to their former bloodthirsty selves."

"Yes," said Dr. Broth. "And we must return to the twenty-first century. Who knows who might be thumbing through my manuscript even as we speak."

Bidding their respective adieus, Dr. Mesmer and the three time travelers went their separate ways: Mesmer into the street, and Dr. Broth, Ollie, and McGuffin into the ether.

But just as the world began to form out of the hyperhaze, they found themselves hurtling toward the Earth, spiraling out of control.

"Mayday! Mayday!" shouted the alpaca to the wind.

The professor was turning green.

"Where's the airsickness bag?" he yelled.

Luckily an ocean and shoreline appeared beneath them. Ollie took off his scarf and made a small parachute. They glided down to the surface and settled comfortably in the sea.

The three waded through the chest-deep water toward the rocky, barren shore. A large dark shape caught Dr. Broth's eye. "The Statue of Liberty!" he shouted, pointing toward the land.

The crown and torch of Lady Liberty peeked out from the shore, the rest of her deep beneath the sand. As they dragged themselves onto the beach, a second, larger figure came into view.

"What's that behind her?" asked Ollie.

An inordinately hairy arm protruded from the sand, fiercely holding a riding crop. Beneath it was more black hair parted above thick, protruding eyebrows.

"Judging by the coarse hair, the length of the digits on the hand, and the density of the brow ridge, I'd say that's a gigantic half-buried ape," said Dr. Broth.

They'd just spread out to dry themselves on the beach, when they were startled by the sound of galloping. A herd of alpacas approached them along the shore. But the alpacas themselves weren't doing any galloping. They were riding humans and apes.

"Have these slaves rebelled?" their leader addressed McGuffin.

"Slaves? What slaves?" answered McGuffin.

"An animal-rights enthusiast, eh?" said the leader. "Round 'em all up!"

At once the alpacas dismounted from the primates, and before they knew what was going on, the trio was in shackles.

"Where on Earth did these oddballs come from?" said the leader's second-in-command out of the side of his mouth. "It's like they fell out of the sky."

They marched them over the rocks along the shore, across open fields, past rows of man and ape—side by side and chained together—laying down the magnetic rails for a levitating train line. Here and there, humans and apes could be seen tilling the fields of alfalfa plantations and milling around in corrals. Then they passed through barren stretches of land, which eventually turned into a dusty city buzzing with the sound of teenage alpacas on

their floating skateboards. The doctor, Ollie, and McGuffin were brought directly to the central part of the city: the district prison. After leading them through a labyrinth of increasingly dark, dank corridors, two burly guards threw them into a tiny cell.

The three time travelers sat fuming behind bars.

"I knew I should have enslaved you," said McGuffin, "then I'd be sitting pretty right now."

"There's got to be some way outta here," said Dr. Broth, giving the handle of the door a twist.

Then they noticed that in the opposite cell, an ape was waving his food tray at them. On the tray were a series of dents, possibly made with the wrong end of a fork. The rooms, apparently, were soundproof—they could hear nothing outside their cell.

"What do you think that ape's trying to tell us?" asked McGuffin.

"It's a strange pattern," said Dr. Broth. "Perhaps a cross between the Inca counting method and the code used among sailors during the Fifty-seven Years War. Just a moment." He went over

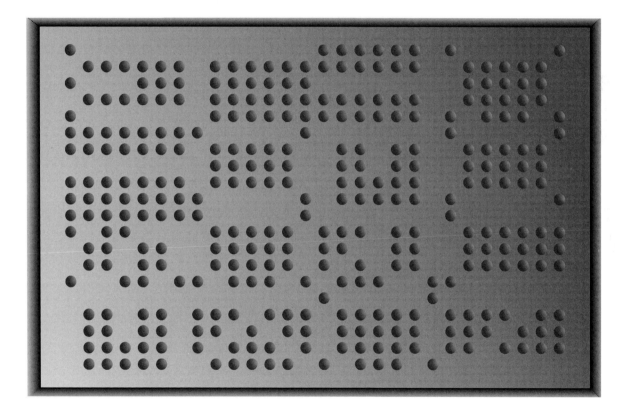

to the wall, and, using his own fork, began to bang out little dents in an attempt to decipher the code.

"You don't need to ruin the fork," said Ollie. "I think I see what that ape is trying to tell us."

Cell Walls

THE CAPTIVES STEPPED OUT of their cell as quietly as possible. Immediately, they understood why it had been so easy for the ape to help them: The alpaca warden had left the key in their door. They padded down the gloomy halls, with gloomy rooms on either side of them. Many of them contained a rebellious or free-spirited animal of some kind. A peacock paced defiantly in one; a lethargic platypus lay sprawled on his cot in another. They passed a caddish skink chucking cards into a pot, and a wild-eyed bush baby rattled a tin can against the bars of his cage. After a few turns down a few hallways, they realized that they didn't know where they were.

"Maybe we should backtrack and see if that ape can help us," said Ollie.

But as soon as they'd turned around, they found that they'd lost all sense of direction.

"In a perfect mathematical world," said Dr. Broth, "all mazes are solvable: Simply take a left at every opportunity. If a turn becomes a dead end, backtrack and continue until you reach another fork or decision, then keep sticking to the left. It may take some time, but eventually it will work."

They put Dr. Broth's plan into practice. But left after left, animal criminal after animal criminal, they still had seen no signs of the exit.

A nutria threw some muck at them.

"Somehow," said the McGuffin, "I don't think this is the perfect mathematical world you had in mind."

Hours passed. Then suddenly they were back where they started.

"That was a nice evening stroll. Shall we retire?" asked McGuffin.

Ollie ran to the ape and asked if he knew how to get out of the place. The ape waddled to the back of his cell and came back with sixteen cards.

"After having seen a few of the hallways in this place, I've cobbled together this unique map. Each card is a view of a hallway. You can tell from the following card which door you ought to have taken to get to the hallway it depicts. It's fairly obvious—just follow the cards from hallway to hallway. You probably didn't realize that there are several floors to this place, so be sure to pay attention to trap doors in the ceil-

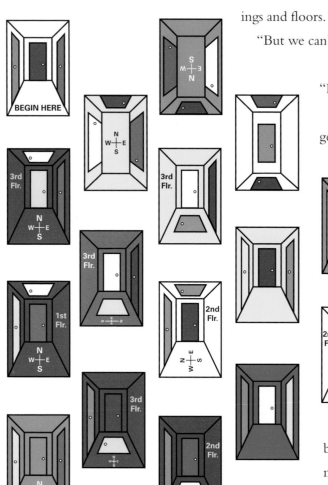

ings and floors. I wish you the best of luck."

"But we can't take this from you," said Ollie.

McGuffin and Dr. Broth looked at each other. "Lost his mind," mouthed McGuffin.

"It's probably taken you years to put this together, and it's surely your one hope of escape," said Ollie.

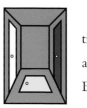

"All we have to do is wait around till the alpaca is 'feeling comfortable,' and we can get out of here," said Dr. Broth.

"Oh, don't worry about that," said the ape. "I quite like it here. Food's O.K., they've got a nice gym, and the library's really fantastic. You see, I'm not quite right in the head and wouldn't do too well out there. Plus, with all this time on my hands, I've been able to help the folks at Oxford with etymologies for their new Alpaca-English dictionary. Anyway, I've got those cards memorized by now."

So they sauntered on after a heartfelt offering of thanks.

". . . helping the folks at Oxford, eh? Let me see those cards," said the doctor, trying to grab them from Ollie's hands. Instead, the cards flew into the air and ended up scattered all over the floor.

"Now, how are we going to get out of this zoo from hell?" asked McGuffin.

Ollie calmly gathered the cards from the ground. "Don't worry," he said, "there's only one way these cards can be arranged that makes any sense."

Spitmus Test

FINALLY THEY SPOTTED SUNLIGHT shining through the exit. Outside, an alpaca stood guard on either side of the door.

"What should we do?" asked Ollie.

"Why, there's nothing for it," said McGuffin. "You'll have to put me on your shoulders."

So with Ollie hunched over in front and Dr. Broth bringing up the rear, they passed through the gate with McGuffin on their shoulders.

"Halt! Who goes there?" asked one of the guards.

"Stand and unfold yourself!" said the other.

"I don't think it's possible with all this weight on my back," said Ollie.

"Quiet, fool!" shouted McGuffin, giving Ollie a kick in the ribs. "I'm taking these criminals to be executed."

"Where are the papers? You know no one can leave the prison without papers," said the first guard.

"Papers? Ah, oh, papers. In this case the orders are from very high up, very high up. 'No papers,' I was told. 'Absolutely no papers.' So, ah, I'm very sorry, there are, no papers at this time. If you have any problems with that, well, ask, ah, you-know-who. That's what he told me to say. When you ask for the papers."

"Sounds pretty suspicious to me," said the second guard.

"Yeah. That's pretty weak. What should we do with 'em?"

"I suppose we should arrest 'em and toss 'em in solitary confinement."

"Ah, God! And fill out all that paperwork? You really wanna be here till two in the morning?"

"Got a better idea?"

"Sure, take their word for it."

"We'll be in the dung heap when their cell's found empty."

"Did you forget? We're subbing for Ross and Finestein—off the record. It's their problem."

Dr. Broth's knees were wobbling as he got closer and closer to the ground.

"Don't just stand there," said the first guard, "beat it while you got a chance."

A Courageous Escape

129

So Dr. Broth and Ollie shuffled off as quickly as possible. They passed a few corners and found themselves in the city square.

"Can we put you down now?" asked Ollie.

"Quiet, fool!" shouted McGuffin. "Slaves don't speak till spoken to." And then in a hushed voice, "No, I can't let you down. Do you see any other apes or humans walking around without alpacas on their backs? Do you wanna get killed?"

In the square there was a crowd watching some kind of sporting event.

"Take me over there," demanded McGuffin.

At the crowd's edge, McGuffin peeped over the heads of other alpacas propped on other primates. In front of them was a long stretch of land. A row of alpacas waited behind a chalk mark on the ground. About fifty feet from the chalk line was a glass square with a black frame painted on it. Behind this glass was some kind of camera; above it, an LCD.

A burly alpaca wearing high boots and purple spandex, with a black star painted on his face, sauntered up to the chalk mark. A man approached him with a piece of watermelon. The beast took a bite from the wedge, chewed, sucked, chewed, then sucked before assuming an athletic pose. Then he pulled his head back as far as possible and threw it forward, spitting with all his might. A black seed streaked through the air. There was a sharp ping as it hit the glass and *85 MPH* appeared on the LCD.

"Giant Lemuel Gulletver, though clocking in at an impressive eighty-five miles per hour, has just missed the square," announced a booming voice. "I'm afraid that means he's out of the spit game with no chance of making it into the finals. Very tough break for this rookie sensation from Chile."

Gulletver stormed off to the sidelines, pounding his hooves on the dirt in rage.

"Now here's the unstoppable Garglantua." An even larger alpaca with long mangy wool, a hoop earring in his ear, and a tattoo of a sexy alpaca on his shoulder stepped up to the chalk line. Another man approached him with a wedge of watermelon, and the brute took a bite with a growl. Then he whipped his head back and threw forward a powerful spit.

Few in the crowd saw the seed at all. There was a loud crash, and the alpacas went wild as they realized that the powerful Garglantua had shattered the target.

The LCD read *102*.

"One hundred and two! One hundred and two! An in-*cred*-ible shot! Is it? Yes! A new speed record! The fastest spit ever recorded! But how can we go on without a target?!" spouted the sports announcer. "The target, which is meant to break along certain lines in a case like this, hasn't broken since the year 4552, when Loogie Gehrig broke the target *and* the world record. So we appreciate your patience while we try to fit the pieces back together."

"Pieces like that keep cropping up everywhere we go," said McGuffin.

Ollie was studying the ground intently.

"Excuse me," he said. And everyone immediately looked at him with disgust. Slaves, it seemed, weren't supposed to speak.

"Excuse me, but I think I see a way to put your target back together."

Splattered

THE ALPACAS, AFTER THEIR initial revulsion upon hearing a slave speak out of turn, were grateful to have their target restored. When McGuffin saw the look of approval in the crowd, he sent Ollie and Dr. Broth into the field to put the target back together.

Besieged at the Games

"Yep, those are my slaves," McGuffin was saying to the alpacas around him. "Not always as obedient as I'd like but certainly useful."

Out in the field, Ollie squatted around the pieces, carefully placing them in the right configuration. Dr. Broth stared at two pieces in his hands.

"Can I have that one on the left?" asked Ollie. "It goes right here."

"Oh, yes, of course," said Dr. Broth, snapping out of his trance. "I was just examining the execution of the weak lines. They seemed to have effectuated stress points in a fairly efficacious manner. All the structural tension is focused on what are now the edges of these pieces. When aligned, that tension is entirely transparent, except for a slight shift in chirality. Perhaps if we had a polarized ultraviolet light . . ."

Ollie grabbed the pieces out of Dr. Broth's hands.

"Do you think you could see if anyone has any twine or rubber bands? I need to hold everything together while I fit the last two pieces in."

The doctor stood up and turned to the crowd.

"Excuse me, we need a piece of twine to complete our repairs. Do any of you llamas—"

The doctor never finished his sentence. A storm of spit-fire descended upon him. Every alpaca, from the old-timers on the sidelines and the children in the front row to the contestants and McGuffin, sent a saliva sample the doctor's way. But it was Garglantua himself who did the doctor in. He'd been sucking on a jawbreaker after his triumphant trajectory when he heard the fateful word, and he immediately sent it toward Dr. Broth at 102 miles per hour. It ricocheted off Dr. Broth's forehead amidst the barrage of spit, and he fell to the ground unconscious.

"Oh, lordy!" shouted Ollie as he and McGuffin ran forward.

Ollie looked around for a stretcher, but the only thing he could find was the target's cover.

"That won't work," said McGuffin, "his legs'll drag off one side and his head off the other."

"If you have a knife, I can turn that square into a rectangle of the same area with two quick cuts."

The Hospittle

DR. BROTH LAY ON his back in the alpaca hospital. The ambulance had tried to take him to the veterinary hospital, but McGuffin had insisted that he get the same care as a free citizen. Dr. Broth had plenty of space in the oversized oval bed. But a great pink knob sat on the middle of his forehead. He was groaning.

"Don't worry, you'll be up and walking in no time," reassured Ollie.

"Though the doctor did say you may be unusually oblivious for a day or two," said McGuffin.

A fluffy white nurse came into the room.

"I'm sorry, but visiting hours are over. You can return tomorrow at four, if you like." She placed a glass of water and two thumb-sized pills next to Dr. Broth's bed.

Ollie and McGuffin filed out and headed toward the waiting room.

"I'm exhausted," said McGuffin.

"So am I," said Ollie. "But we don't really have anywhere to go."

Blankets covered the waiting-room floor.

"We might as well stay here," said McGuffin, "there's no one around, and it looks like we could make ourselves quite comfy."

The pair curled up with a few blankets in a corner and quickly fell asleep.

Shortly before two in the morning, a crash and a few hollers woke the pair. Six drunken alpacas stumbled into the waiting room. Two of them had black eyes, one was missing a tooth, another had a deep cut on his ear, and the last two limped as if they'd broken a bone or two.

"Doctor! I need a doctor!" shouted one of the limping alpacas.

"What's the matter?" asked Ollie.

"What's the matter? I tell you what's the matter. That filthy gang of Chileans ganged up on us! We were outnumbered five to one!"

"Aww, put a cork in it, Jones," said an alpaca with a black eye. "We was whupped and that's all there is to it."

"We got our tails shorn, for sure," said the alpaca with the cut ear, "but I'll be a camel if we didn't smash every piece of glass in the place."

A nurse appeared behind the waiting-room counter.

"You guys back again so soon?"

"We don't need to hear anything from you," said Jones. "Just send us a doctor."

The nurse grumbled a bit before picking up the phone. He scribbled a few things on a piece of paper and then hung up.

"I'm sorry," he said, "but there's only one doctor on duty right now. He'll see each of you one at a time." The nurse pushed the schedule he'd written across the counter:

Smith: 2:00–2:30

Kwan: 2:30–3:30

Jones: 3:30–4:15

Quartey: 4:15–4:35

Williams: 4:35–4:50

Gupta: 4:50–5:30

"I only get twenty minutes?" said Quartey.

"You've got a cut on your ear, for crying out loud. We ought to send you home to have Mommy kiss it," said the nurse.

"I've got to wait more than two and a half hours," said Williams.

"And I'll be sitting here for nearly three," said Gupta.

"This is outrageous!" shouted Kwan. "The average wait for the six of us is ninety-six minutes."

Ollie had been watching from his corner. "Excuse me," he said, "but if you just rearrange the names you can cut the average waiting time to less than ninety minutes."

"Don't help them," whispered McGuffin, "they're liable to tear our heads off."

"If we can get a few of them out of here sooner, we stand a chance of getting some sleep."

Gypsy Geography

"HEY SLAVE," SHOUTED JONES to Ollie, as Ollie was dozing off again.

"Yes?" said Ollie nervously.

"You really helped us save ourselves some time. Is there anything we can do to help you out?"

"Why, yes," said Ollie, gaining confidence. "As a matter of fact, we're fugitives and—"

"Outlaws?"

"Well, yes."

"Why didn't you say so? We'll help you get out of here."

"Getting out of here isn't the hard part, actually," said Ollie, and he went on to explain their difficulties in finding Dr. Broth's manuscript.

Jones pondered the problem for a moment.

"What you need," he said, "is a visit to Carny Tulip."

At the sound of the name *Carny Tulip* all the rough alpacas started cheering.

When the doctor had seen everyone, the alpacas led Ollie and McGuffin through the dark streets of the city to a door with the words *Fortunes told: $5* painted on it.

"She does her best work at this hour," said Jones.

Inside, Carny Tulip, an extremely furry alpaca with a bandanna wrapped around her ears and forehead, sat in front of a TV and a crystal ball.

"Hey, Carny," said Jones as they barged in, "can you do a favor for us? These hardened criminals here could use your advice."

Carny Tulip looked up at them with her heavy-lidded eyes and didn't say a word. She motioned for Ollie to sit across from her. When he'd explained their predicament, she brought out a bag and a strange circular grid.

"In this bag," she said softly, "are all the regions of the world, old and new. Reach in and pull out twenty-seven names."

When Ollie had done this, she lined up the twenty-seven names and instructed him to choose a city from each region and put it in the grid in order. Each name, she said, would share at least one letter with the name before it and the name after it. When he'd filled in every square, the letters in the box would tell him where to go.

1. Venezuela
2. Wyoming
3. Australia
4. Ontario
5. New Jersey
6. Switzerland
7. Colorado
8. Michigan
9. Italy
10. Japan
11. Burkina Faso
12. Netherlands
13. Syria
14. Spain
15. England
16. Brazil
17. Togo
18. California
19. Ancient Greece
20. Nigeria
21. Morocco
22. Germany
23. Uganda
24. Lebanon
25. Tunisia
26. South Vietnam
27. Ethiopia

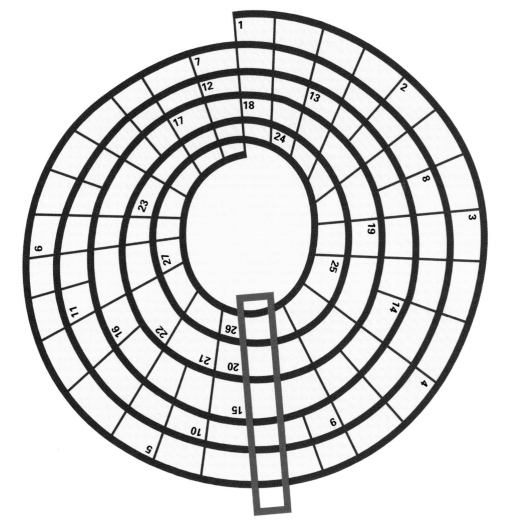

Ollie and McGuffin chose the places and pored over the names. The toughs helped them out where they could, and it wasn't long before Ollie knew where to head next. It was now daylight. Ollie and McGuffin thanked everyone and hurried back to Dr. Broth.

They found him counting the ways to divide the hospital window.

Lost in Space-time

WHEN DR. BROTH HAD recuperated and McGuffin was finally feeling "at ease," the three adventurers left the Planet of the Alpacas for the infinitesimal dimension.

As they jetted through the ether, a strange form emerged. At first it seemed just a speck, then an

A Gentleman Space Traveler

overfed speck. Eventually they could make out a man in an antiquated spacesuit, with a monocle in his right eye and a cane in his right hand, floating toward them, reading the paper.

"Good evening, my friends," he said, when they were at a polite speaking distance. "Nice weather we're having, isn't it?"

"Sure," said McGuffin, "but it isn't evening. The sun's usually up out here."

"Ah, yes. I'm afraid I still go by the time back home at Blount Nebula. A little nostalgic tic of mine, I suppose. And what brings you fine people out today?"

"We're searching for my life's work," said Dr. Broth. "It was misplaced by the airline company when I was returning from a conference on astro—"

"What about you?" interrupted Ollie.

"I'm in a bit of a bind myself," said the man. "My twin—fraternal—and I left home about the same time and went our separate ways. But before we parted, we agreed that we'd meet again on our thirty-eighth birthday. But while we're traveling about at the speed of light, we don't age. I've traveled two extra light years, so even though I've just turned thirty-six, he's turning thirty-eight at this very instant. I still have a chance of meeting him when we're both thirty-eight, provided that he continues traveling at the speed of light and we meet at the right place and time."

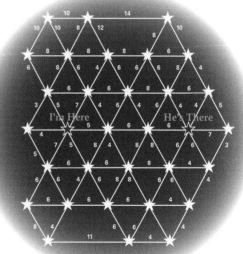

"And how do you plan to do that?" asked Dr. Broth.

"That's the problem. I've just been bouncing around from star to star in this blighted galaxy. It does have its attractions, but there's plenty of dead space. I was hoping I'd just run into him. But even if that should happen, there's no way of being sure we'll both be thirty-eight."

Ollie took a look at the map of stars the man was carrying.

"I think I see what star you should head for and how to get there," said Ollie. "We'll have to assume your brother figures out the right path as well."

"Or finds someone like you to explain it to him," said the man. The distances between stars were marked in light years.

Once upon a Prime in Italy

"NEED I POINT OUT," started Dr. Broth as a group of girls in togas passed by, "that this hardly appears to be twenty-first-century India?"

"What do you mean?" said McGuffin, gazing at the urns the girls carried. "Looks like I've taken you to the biggest toga party in the history of Rajasthan State University."

"Perhaps it's not altogether a surprise," said Broth. "We forgot to factor in continental drift."

The flat, dusty land spread out for miles until it collided with a clump of small mountains. On a narrow path leading up into the hills, a lanky disheveled man appeared, heading their way. They could make out a long unkempt mustache, ragged clothes, and a tall wide-brimmed hat.

"Evening, amigos," he said when at last he came upon them. He wore spurs on his boots and had an empty holster around his waist. "Any ways I can help ya?"

"As a matter of fact, yes," said Dr. Broth. "Do you know what century it is and how we might be able to get out of it?"

"It just so happens that I was ponderin' on that problem this mornin'. Seems like everyone's got their own ideas about it. Back where I come from, people think one thing; but here, they think another. Up north, it's altogether a different story; for some reason they've tacked a few extras on. And those Persians, who think they're something big, they got ideas altogether their own. Personally, I figure time's been going on forever and'll keep on going on forever, so why put too fine a point on it?"

"Perhaps you could tell us," asked Ollie, "who the current king of Rome is?"

"Why, sure. Lucius Tarquinius Superbus. Superbus, I assure you, is just a name."

"That puts us in the fifth century B.C." whispered Dr. Broth.

"I see y'all're number-minded folk, yerselves. Can't help noticing that there's three of ya. Three's the first proper pyramid number, and a very masculine number, too. It's no coincidence that yer all of the male persuasion."

"Just my bad luck," said McGuffin, still looking at the passing maidens. "Could you get me some of those babes' numbers instead?"

"If yer interested," continued the man, "I'm headed to Croton, where I happen to be high sheriff. Right now we're about to start our own Olympics, a kinda number Olympics. Thought we'd put up a

Running into the Law

little competition to the muscle games. If y'all got a mind fer it, maybe y'all can come compete."

"I've always wanted to see how I'd compare to the best minds of ancient Greece and Rome," said Dr. Broth. "Who knows? Maybe we'd get a chance to meet Pythagoras or some other genius."

"Pythagoras: that's ma name—don't wear it out! If y'all have come to join my colony yer in luck. Croton's just a hop and a holler away."

After following Pythagoras, high sheriff of Croton, for several hours, they came upon a fortress. A gigantic flag depicting five interlocking circles hung from its outer wall.

"Look, it's the sign of the Olympics," said McGuffin.

"That's our first contest," said Pythagoras. "Everyone should be working hard on it right now. The idea is to fill every section made by the circles with a number from one to fifteen. The numbers in each circle should add up to a prime number. Then, if it so happens ya can get that far, add up the sum of each circle to get the highest number possible, and that's how we find our winner."

"Why, this is a simple Venn diagram. But the introduction of cortatras to this selection of integers creates a complication. In fact, while there's a finite solution, finding it could require advance—"

"I think," said Ollie as humbly as possible, "I see a winning answer."

The Principles of Seating

"THAT ABOUT SETTLES THAT," said Pythagoras suspiciously. "You folk may want to stick around for the rest of the competition."

Thousands of people were flocking to the compound, many dressed in togas and a few in robes lined with purple. Pythagoras ushered the crew inside the walls to a great stadium, which was quickly filling up. He invited them to sit on the stage among the circle of competitors.

To the right of the stage were thirty-six seats for the purple-clad judges. They milled about from seat to seat, unable to get settled.

"There are two kinds of judges," explained Pythagoras, "the Stoics and the Dionysians. Four of each must sit in the front row. But the Dionysians love diversity and prefer to sit behind one Dionysian and one Stoic. The Stoics, on the other hand, prefer homogeneity and will sit only behind two Stoics or two Dionysians. Aside from the eight judges in the front, there are eleven Stoics and seventeen Dionysians."

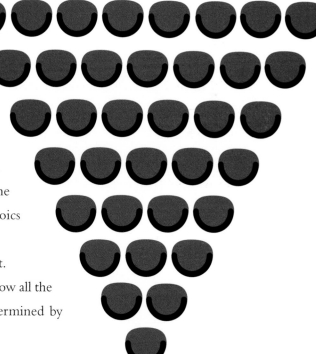

Ollie pondered the problem for a moment.

"There are two configurations that will allow all the judges to have a seat. Naturally, they're determined by those in the first row."

Ordering Off the Menu

WHEN EVERY SEAT IN the amphitheater was taken, Pythagoras motioned for quiet and gave an introductory speech. "And before we begin, let me remind y'all that these numbers are the purest and most spiritual path we can take. Life on this here planet, and elsewhere in the universe, is eternal, and we must always focus on purity. The prime numbers, amigos, are the purest of all numbers. And so, before we begin this most spiritual of contests, let us take a moment to remember the seventeen forbidden foods."

The audience began to recite with him.

"We shall not eat meat of any kind.

"We shall not eat lima beans.

"We shall not eat foods that have been boiled and then roasted.

"We shall not eat pinto beans.

"We shall not eat from a whole loaf of bread.

"We shall not eat kidney beans.

"We shall not eat scrambled eggs.

"We shall not eat garbanzo beans.

"We shall not eat boiled eggs.

"We shall not eat black beans.

"We shall not eat roasted eggs.

"We shall not eat green beans.

"We most definitely shall not eat eggs that have been boiled and then roasted.

"We shall not eat string beans.

"We shall not eat any food that causes flatulence.

"We shall not eat baked beans.

"We shall not eat beans of any kind."

"It's hardly a coincidence, my brothers and sisters, that there are seventeen forbidden foods. Because seventeen is the most divine of all prime numbers. And now for our first ceremonial competition."

A slave in a purple toga brought Pythagoras the frames of three triangles. "These triangles," he explained, "must be arranged, by placing them on top of one another, so that seventeen sections—representing, of course, places for the seventeen forbidden foods—are made by their intersections."

"I don't see how that could possibly . . . ," started Dr. Broth, glancing over at Ollie's wax tablet. Ollie was putting the finishing touches on his sketch of the solution.

Numbers Speak

"I WOULDN'T BE TOO quick with that answer," said McGuffin to Ollie. "These Pythagoreans look like a competitive bunch, and they might not like being outdone by foreigners every time. At least wait till someone else gets close."

Ollie looked around at the other contestants. They were all furiously scribbling away.

"I think you're right," added Dr. Broth, "I'm sure we wouldn't want to add to any inferiority complex they might have by offering a solution at such an early moment. Better we should practice our modesty in the face of such xenophobia."

"*Zeno*-phobia?" said McGuffin. "I don't think these guys have ever gotten *close* to a finish line."

By the time Dr. Broth had finished his humble proposal Ollie had noticed a few competitors with I-think-I've-got-it expressions on their faces. Ollie's hand shot up into the air just before those of several others.

Pythagoras walked over to Ollie who handed him the wax tablet with his answer. Pythagoras examined it for a few moments.

"Well hang my butt in the mulberry tree! You've done it again!" he exclaimed and then turned toward the audience. "*Amigos, romanos, campesinos*: I think we've got a winner."

He looked toward Ollie and his exuberance lessened.

"However, the aforementioned winner is not currently using a number-two stylus. I'm sorry pardner, but I'm gonna have to disqualify ya fer this round."

"Excuse me," said Ollie, "but I don't have a number-two stylus."

"If the contestant does not have a number-two stylus, a number-two stylus will be provided, if requested by said contestant. Rule 32,453, subsection M."

"Then I would like to request a number-two stylus," said Ollie.

A surly judge in a purple-lined toga brought a new stylus to Ollie. As he handed over the stylus, it bounced off Ollie's fingers and fell to the floor. Ollie nervously bent down to pick it up, and everyone in the amphitheater gasped. Sheriff Pythagoras was appalled.

"Now lookee here," he said, "you've gone and broke one of the major tenets of the Pythagorean code: Never pick up anything you've dropped. You've disregarded our customs and disrespected our way of life. Cowboy, I declare you doubly disqualified."

A murmur went through the crowd.

"However," continued Pythagoras, contemplatively rubbing his chin, "seeing as how two negatives make a positive, looks like I have to make ya the winner again."

Everyone applauded as Ollie's face filled with a mixture of blush and bewilderment.

"And now," said Pythagoras, "time for this year's prime-number sentences. I give y'all the sentences—spiritual sentences to reinforce our standards and values—in which each letter represents a prime number. And I don't have to tell you *compadres* that while some of the primes are yer garden-variety primes, some of 'em are gonna be doozies. This here's the Olympics, after all. After a little ciphering, y'all should be able to tell me what number each letter has to be to make the equations work."

The judges brought out four stones with the "sentences" carved into them:

$$ALE = BEE - E$$
$$ALL + BEANS = ARE\ BAD$$
$$METAL \times BEANS = ABSENT\ MEAL$$
$$SEAL + BALL = BAR - JAVA$$

Prime Gears

AFTER OLLIE HAD WON yet again, Pythagoras announced a short intermission, and the competitors filed out of the amphitheater. Outside were hundreds of carts, hawkers, and souvenir stands. The three citizens of the future bought a few dolmas-on-a-stick and strolled through the throng of spectators and contestants.

"Maybe you should stock up on supplies," said McGuffin to Ollie. "You might not want to get caught on another technicality."

They passed a cart filled with tools for the Pythagorean athlete.

"Styli here," called out a barker, "get your styli, counting beans, and Nike tablets. Official wax tablets of the Pythagorean Olympics."

"Uh, I'll take two wax tablets and a stylus," said Ollie.

"And I'll have the same," said Dr. Broth.

"These are number-two styli, aren't they?" asked Ollie.

"Of course, of course. I'm not trying to sell you a handicap," said the salesman.

"I was under the impression," said McGuffin, "that beans were not in favor here. And yet you're selling them in broad daylight."

Treats from Street Vendors

"Why, we've got nothing against beans. Beans are a thing of nature. How could we add or subtract without beans? No, we like beans. But beans are for counting, not for eating!"

"I guess that's using your bean," said McGuffin.

"Perhaps you could tell me," said Ollie as he handed over a few obols, "what contest is next on the schedule?"

"Of course, of course. It's right here on the program." The salesman pulled a scroll from under his table. "Next is the great hexagonathon. You don't look like you're from around here. Are you contestants?"

"I suppose we are," said Ollie.

"Well then, you'll need to buy some hexagons, too." The salesman reached under his table again and came up with three small bags. He handed one to each of the time travelers.

Inside every bag were seven small hexagons. Each hexagon had the numbers one, two, three, five, and seven on different sides, with one side left blank.

Once they'd consumed their dolmas-on-a-stick, they sauntered back to their positions in the amphitheater. Pythagoras took the stage when everyone had settled, and then he called for their attention. Behind him stood seven wooden hexagons, each four feet high, with the same numbers carved in them as those in the hexagons Ollie, McGuffin, and Dr. Broth had in their bags.

"It's time for the hexagonathon, friends. This time the problem's simple. Place these hexagons in a group, six of them around a seventh in the center, so that all the numbers created where sides meet are prime. Take all the time y'all want. If and when someone thinks he's got an answer, come on down here and try it out on the big display."

As soon as the words were out of his mouth, all the contestants had brought out their hexagons and started arranging them.

"I think I have an answer," said Ollie to Dr. Broth after a few minutes. "But I may need your help moving those big hexagons."

Takes a Licking, Keeps on Casting a Shadow

"I THINK WE'VE GOT a solution," called Ollie across the crowd to Pythagoras.

"Well then, step right up and give us all a look-see on the big hexes here."

Ollie and Dr. Broth climbed on stage and tried their best to raise the hexagons on top of one another against the wall. Moving one took all the strength the two of them had. They were too pooped to move any of the others.

"Do you mind if we use the assistance of our friend?" asked Dr. Broth.

"What am I, a mule?" muttered McGuffin.

Pythagoras motioned him on stage.

"Pickle my hog's feet!" said Pythagoras when he saw their answer. "These foreign folk done did it again. Let's just see how y'all do on the next one."

"Don't you think we should be departing soon?" Dr. Broth asked Ollie, with a glance at his watch.

"How'd you know?" asked Pythagoras. He looked at his watch, too: a coin-sized sundial on his wrist. "It's time for the time puzzle."

"Where did you get that watch?" asked Dr. Broth.

"Why, do you like it?"

"It's very nice, but none of the sundials that have survived into our time predate the third century."

"This is a Babylonian import—very rare." Sheriff Pythagoras was getting contemplative again. He rubbed his chin.

Ollie, Dr. Broth, and McGuffin returned to their seats.

"Take a look at this timepiece," said Pythagoras as he walked among the contestants. "On it are twelve numbers representing the twelve hours of the half day. Divide the face of this dial into three sections so that the numbers of each section add up to a prime number."

"Actually," said Ollie, "there are two solutions."

Astral Travel Agency

PYTHAGORAS PLACED THE CROWN of wild olive on Ollie's head. The audience admired the ritual in silence—clapping hadn't yet been invented.

"No, I never woulda thought I'd come across a mind like yers. If there's anything I can do to help ya in yer journeys, just let me know."

Ollie was feeling exhausted. "Actually, I think you could help us. Do you happen to know anyone who could tell us where we should be going and how we should get there?"

"Know anyone? I've started my own travel agency/astrology service to help out wanderers like ourselves. It's called Oracle Travel."

When the crowd had thinned out, the town criers had finished their interviews, and Ollie had turned down several offers from various sandal manufacturers, Pythagoras led them to a stone observatory on a hill in the outskirts of Croton. There they met the soothsayer/astronomer: an excited woman with thick, dexterous eyebrows.

"These brilliant friends of mine have just won the Olympics," said Pythagoras. "They were hoping ya could get them to where they're going."

"Where *are* they going?" she asked with a furrow.

"That's just the problem," jumped in Dr. Broth. "We need to find a piece of luggage of mine that's floating around somewhere in the twenty-first century."

"That'll be no problem at all. Nebulous travel is our specialty," she said, and led them inside.

Charts of the constellations covered all the walls; notched sticks of various sizes stood in the corners; and the absence of a roof allowed for contemplation of the stars. The travel agent/priestess sat Dr. Broth in the center of the room. Before he had a chance to ask what was going on, she ripped a few hairs from his head.

"Ow! What did you do that for?"

"Hold on and you'll see," she said, arching the heavy fur above her right eye. She threw the hairs onto a table, blew on them, and then poured wax from a burning candle onto the center of the table. Then she peered up at the sky. Stars were just beginning to emerge. On a gridded piece of papyrus she began to scrawl numbers. She glanced back at the stars and scrawled a few more numbers. She repeated this procedure several times and then turned to her clients.

"This tells where your luggage is," she said, and handed Dr. Broth the papyrus.

He studied the numbers and the empty grid.

"I don't understand. Where is the luggage?"

"I don't know," she said, waggling her eyebrows. "But if you fill in the grid according to the numbers, it will show two images that will reveal all. The numbers followed by an *R* tell you how many red squares there are in that row or column of the grid. Numbers followed by a *B* tell you how many blue squares are in the row or column. Numbers followed by a *P* tell you how many purple squares there are in a row or column. The purple is where the two images overlap."

Column clues (top to bottom within each column):

```
                                        3R
                                  3R    1P
                      4B    1B                1R
          4R 3R 1R 1B 1P 5B 1B 2R 2R 3R 2P 3B 3R 3R 3R 2R 2R 1R 4B
 3R 4R 5R 1P 2P 18P 16P 11P 10P 9P 6P 7P 7P 1B 3P 5B 2B 2B 3B 4B 5B 2R
 4B 6B 8B 13B 14B 1B 4B 6B 8B 5B 5B 3B 1B 5P 2R 5R 8R 7R 5R 5R 6R 2R 2B
```

Row clues (top to bottom):

Row clue
3R 2B
4R 3B
5R 2B
5R 2B
3R 2P 3B
7P 12R
3B 3P 2P 10R 2B
4B 7P 6R 3B
4B 10P 7B
5B 9P 8B
5B 8P 3B 3B
5B 9P 2B 2B
1B 3B 10P 1B
3B 5P 1B 4P 1R
2B 4P 3B 3P 2R
2B 3P 5B 1P 4R
2B 3P 4B 8R
2B 3P 3B 7R
2B 2P 3B 5R
1B 2P 2B 5R
1B 1P 3B 6R
1P 3B 2R 2R
4B
2B

Mangled Motto

"SO WE HAVE TO figure out our own itinerary?" asked Dr. Broth.

"That's right."

". . . which is determined by the stars?"

"Correct. And we've never had an unhappy customer. It's all in our motto." She pointed to three interlocking hexagons filled with seemingly random hexagons.

"Somehow I'm not reassured," said Dr. Broth.

"Oh, sorry, I didn't notice," said the woman. "Those magpies must have turned the wheels again. Each wheel has been turned once, actually. Our motto is made up of three twelve-letter words. The words have common letters where the wheels intersect. That's why three twelve-letter words fit onto the thirty hexagons that make the wheels. Give me a moment and I'll fix it so you can see."

"That's O.K.," said Ollie, "I can tell what the words are."

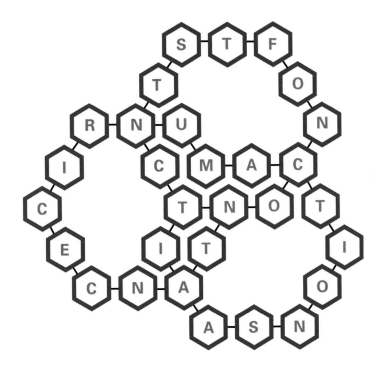

India Air

"WHAT'S THAT SMELL?" asked McGuffin, trying to hold his nose with his hooves. They had landed on a runway at some Indian international airport.

"Smells like methane to me," said Ollie.

"Actually, methane has no intrinsic odor," said Dr. Broth. "What you smell is the bacterial decomposition of cow patties, which are a major source of fuel for India's poor. In fact, cow—"

A plane landed a few feet away and blew them into a ditch beside the runway.

"Perhaps we should go inside," suggested Ollie.

They scurried about the runway, dodging flights and flight attendants, until they reached the airport. A group of travelers just off a 747 were filing inside. The time travelers jumped into line and followed them all the way to customs.

"Look," said Ollie, pointing to a giant clock on the wall.

"Can it be?" asked Dr. Broth.

"What? What's so great about that clock?" said McGuffin.

"It's the time," said Ollie, "you actually seem to have brought us to the right time."

McGuffin looked hurt. "Nothing unusual about that."

"And we do seem to have arrived on the right date," said Dr. Broth, checking a newspaper. "But where are we?"

"Is this your first time in India?" asked the customs woman, beckoning them to her.

"No, it's not," said Dr. Broth, handing her his passport, "but it may be my first time in . . ."

"In where?" she asked.

"In, er . . ."

"At Palam International Airport?"

"No, no, I mean, yes, I've never been there, or here, before."

The customs official eyed his passport suspiciously, then stamped it with a shrug and handed it back.

"Is this your first time in India?" she asked McGuffin as he slid her his passport.

"Absolutely."

"You look much younger in this picture," she said as she stamped his passport and shuffled him through.

"And you, sir. Is this your first time in India?"

"Yes it is, why do you ask?" said Ollie.

"We like to serve our visitors as best we can. Do you need any information?"

"Perhaps you could tell us what city we're in?"

"Did you get on the wrong plane?"

"I don't think so, but it's happened before, and I'd just like to be sure."

"Well, you've arrived in New Delhi. I hope that's where you were trying to go," she said as she stamped Ollie's passport with a whack.

"As a matter of fact it was," said Ollie with a smile.

"It was only a matter of time," said McGuffin.

"Oh, could you tell us where the lost-luggage office is?" asked Ollie before walking away.

"Most definitely. Just follow the ovals on the floor. On each oval is a number. Move ahead that number of ovals horizontally or vertically. You can make turns between ovals, but always move along the lines and never retrace your steps. You'll be led to the right door at the floor's edge in just six moves."

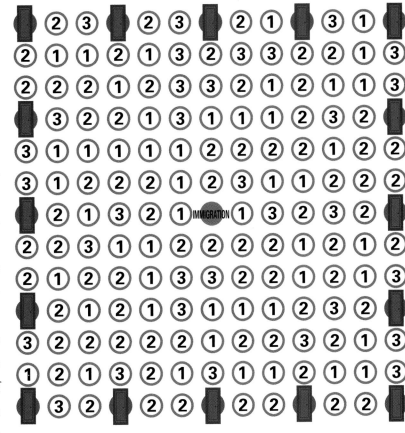

A Brief Case of Mistaken Identity

"HMMMM," SAID THE BESPECTACLED man behind the counter of Palam Airport's lost-luggage office. "Was it a heavy brown attaché case, a little worn, with a leather handle, dull brass clasps, a frayed border on either side, no side pockets, about half a foot wide—"

"Yes, that's it, that it!" shouted Dr. Broth.

"I believe we forwarded the piece to it's owner last night. If it didn't arrive, perhaps we can—"

"But I'm the owner!" shouted Dr. Broth.

"Well, let me check my records. One moment." The man went through a door in the back of the office and quickly returned with a tall ledger. He opened it up before them and ran his finger down the yellow page.

"Yes, right here. One piece of luggage went out last night to a Dr. Brothergee of Lucknow in Uttar Pradesh."

"Brothergee?! The luggage belongs to Dr. Broth. There's no *gee*. I'm him. I'm Dr. Broth. How on Earth did you send it to Dr. Brothergee when it says Dr. Broth right there on the tag?"

"I'm very sorry, sir. It's actually coming back to me now. When I saw the package, I thought it was very odd for us to receive something for a Dr. Broth—I've never come across the name before, you see. I thought perhaps it was a mistake. I looked up Broth in the telephone directory, and the nearest thing to it was Dr. Brothergee."

"And so you just sent it to him?"

"Well, no. Just to be sure, I inspected the contents. And when I found that it was a discourse on non-Euclidean paleolinguistic astrohistoriography, I knew—or thought—it had to belong to our famous non-Euclidean paleolinguistic astrohistoriographist Dr. Brothergee. Please accept my apologies. I'll give you his address so you can pick up the briefcase. I'm sure he'd be delighted to make your acquaintance."

THE TRAVELERS WAITED IN the crowded Old Delhi station for the train to Lucknow. As annoyed as Dr. Broth was at having just missed his luggage, he was excited to think his life's work would soon be in his possession—and perhaps he could discuss some salient points with Dr. Brothergee. The announcement of a stationwide delay did not please him. He wanted to pace, but bodies surrounded him on every side.

"Is there anything we can do to get our train going?" said Dr. Broth to no one in particular.

"I'll go see," said Ollie.

After threading through the throng of waiting passengers Ollie found the switch operator.

"What's the matter?" he asked.

"All the trains have come in at once," said the switch operator, grateful to talk to someone who wasn't yelling at him. "The train from Madras is heading to Calcutta; the train from Bangalore is going to Madras; the train from Delhi is going to Lucknow; the train from Lucknow is going to Bombay; the train from Bombay is going to Bangalore; and the train from Calcutta is going to Delhi. You can see that each section of track can hold one train. The turnaround can hold two cars and the engine of a train. The engines can couple with cars in front as well as behind. We're trying to figure out a way to get each train on its way, but it's very complicated. I am not a happy switch operator, sir. I will be fired and my mother will say, 'Ravi, you are no good.' "

Ollie looked across the tracks. "I think you can get all the trains on their right track, though it will take some time, Ravi," he said.

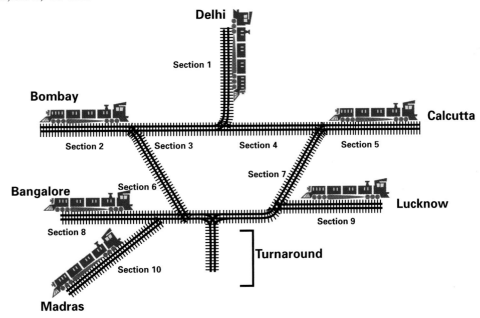

Double, Double, Tile and Trouble

OLLIE ROUNDED UP HIS friends and led them to the platform where the Lucknow-bound train would soon arrive. "If they've followed my instructions, the train should be here any minute," he said.

Sure enough, their train rolled in moments later. But instead of showing any sign of relief or excitement, McGuffin and Dr. Broth looked appalled.

On the Train to Lucknow

"We can't get on there," said Dr. Broth.

"We can't *fit* on there," said McGuffin.

Human bodies filled every inch of the train's floor and many inches that were not the train's floor. People hung from the windows, dangled from the doorways by the dozens, sat on the roof, and clung to any bar or protrusion.

"When they said the trains were filled to a four-hundred-percent capacity, I thought they were talking about the fuel," said McGuffin.

"There must be another train after this one that—" but before Dr. Broth had finished his sentence, a hundred hands picked him up off the platform and pulled him onto the train. Ollie and McGuffin were astonished that they'd made room for Dr. Broth. In a moment they, too, were whisked onto the now-moving train.

"There is room for everyone," said a smiling man pressed against Ollie's side.

Thirteen sweaty hours later, the train arrived at Lucknow, and they waved a sad good-bye to their close new friends Baldev, Dhriti, Oojan, Pratigya, Madhu, Upama, Daya, Bandhura, Kamal, Jayanti, Ushapati, Yogita, Samarat, Madhuri, Lalitesh, Harshita, Champak, Kasturi, Lipika, Induj, Haresh, Gayatri, Phoolendu, Tusti, Chandani, Ambu, Eshwar, Rajkumar, Nandita, Gajanan, Indulala, Rujula, Ujjwal, Subhaga, Tarkesh, Naagesh, Vidhut, Vallabh, Ecchumati, Panduranga, and Jagatprakash. They hailed a cab and sat squashed together, elbow to elbow. But after the crowded train, the backseat felt as spacious as an ocean liner.

Dr. Brothergee lived near the university in a small one-story house secluded by hedges. Dr. Broth rapped on the door and waited. They heard shuffling, and soon a little man in a white suit with a long white beard opened the door.

"Dr. Brothergee?" asked Dr. Broth.

"Yes. That's me."

"I'm Dr. Broth. I've reason to believe—"

"Did you say Dr. Broth?"

"Yes."

"*The* Dr. Broth? Professor of non-Euclidean paleolinguistic astrohistoriographysiology?"

"No, not so specialized. Astrohistoriography is more my line. I was told—"

"I am so honored to be standing here before you, sir. Please come in. I heard you gave quite a talk at the 4,532nd annual convention. I would have been there myself, of course, but the university finance office will only approve trips to international conferences, not intergalactic ones."

Dr. Brothergee seated his guests in an airy living room and went to prepare tea. When he returned, Dr. Broth was quick to speak.

"You're very kind, doctor, but before we continue chatting, could I first address a small concern of mine? You see I—"

"The truncated-thermacline problem?" interrupted Dr. Brothergee, "I'm afraid I go with the classical model on that one. I know it may surprise you, but an intelligent man knows when to take two steps backward to take one step forward. For instance, imagine the forespot of a hariofoid—separate from the body for the sake of argument. . . ."

DR. BROTHERGEE SPOKE WITHOUT pause in such technical detail and without any clear direction that soon even Dr. Broth became drowsy. He'd been holding a cup of tea an inch from his lips, trying to stay awake, when his lids finally closed on him. The teacup fell from his hands, spilling hot tea all over his leg and the carpet. He leapt up in pain and embarrassment and immediately began to apologize to Dr. Brothergee. The carpet looked stained.

"Oh, it's no problem at all," said Dr. Brothergee, "the carpet is made of square tiles and I know where I can order more."

Ollie scrutinized the pattern of dots on the carpet as he tried to mop up what tea he could.

"These are tiles?" he asked. "Where does one end and another begin?"

"Come to think of it, I don't quite remember. I believe they were laid down randomly," said Dr. Brothergee. "There are four different tiles, that much I know."

"That makes it easier," said Ollie. "Now I can see how many tiles have been ruined and their shapes."

"Wonderful," said Dr. Brothergee. "Now where was I? Oh yes. Formalist Mombasa derivations. I'm afraid you can't just throw out the oletrino theory altogether. There's just too many discrepancies that answer to it. . . ."

A thousand daydreams and half a dozen cups of tea later, Ollie suggested that they find some nourishment, not having eaten during any of their recent travels.

"Oh, my! Please forgive me," said Dr. Brothergee. "How rude of me. Unfortunately, I have very little food in the house. If you don't mind a short walk, we can pick up some groceries in the market."

Dr. Brothergee put away the tea things, and they headed out of the house. As they left McGuffin gave Dr. Broth a nudge. In the corner behind the door was a faded leather briefcase, somehow familiar now even to Ollie and McGuffin.

"Wha-Wha-What's this?" said Dr. Broth, lurching toward the corner. He fell onto his knees and started to undo the clasps.

"That," said Dr. Brothergee, "is an enigma. It was delivered to me this morning. An empty briefcase. I don't know why it was sent to me. Perhaps the delivery boy stole the contents."

Ollie and McGuffin were too hungry to give much pause to Dr. Broth's sorrow, so they dragged him along to the market. Dr. Brothergee prated on all the way there and the dazed Dr. Broth stared into space, saying nothing. McGuffin tried to reassure him that they would find the thief somehow.

Fruit with a Peel

THE MARKET WAS IN a small crowded square. Blankets covered every bit of ground, where vendors were selling everything from mango pickle to beetlenut.

"Now be sure to eat only fruit that you peel yourself," advised Dr. Brothergee. "We'll have to get some limes for some limeade."

They approached a woman who sold limes displayed in a pyramid on a rickety table.

"The side of the base of that pyramid is five limes long, so there must be twenty-five limes on the bottom, sixteen in the next row, nine in the middle row, four in the penultimate row and one on top. Fifty-five all together," said Dr. Brothergee proudly. He bought ten limes.

The lime lady looked at her now-imperfect pyramid sadly.

"Don't worry," said Ollie, "your remaining limes can still make one perfect geometric shape with one lime on the top row. It will be like a pyramid, but with a different number of sides. Unfortunately, there will be three limes left over."

"If you can make such a shape," said the lime lady, "I will give you the three extra limes."

A Slash for the Pan

"A FEW LIMES WON'T BE enough for dinner," said Dr. Brothergee. "Let's pick up some sole."

Ollie and McGuffin pulled Dr. Broth through the crowded market. Every time someone with a brief-case walked by, Dr. Broth gave a pained yelp. Ollie and McGuffin had to dig their feet into the dirt to pull him along.

The fish stand was even more crowded than the lime stand had been. People yelled out orders for cod, loach, or yellowtail, and the vendor wrapped orders in two seconds and hurled them at the buyers.

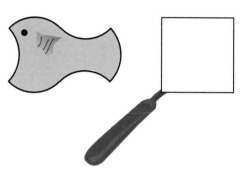

"That's a lotta fish," said McGuffin, slapping his lips.

"Yes," said Dr. Brothergee, "but none of it will do."

"What's the matter? It looks good to me," said Ollie.

"I'm sure it's good, it's just too big."

"Don't worry about that. I could eat a hundred of those," said McGuffin.

"I'm sure, I'm sure. But the problem is that I can't fit those fish into my square baking pans. I've got plenty of baking pans, but each one of those fish are longer than the pans I use."

"If you don't mind cutting the fish first," said Ollie, "you can turn any of these fish into a square with two straight cuts."

Then he pointed to a table filled with winged fish. "How about a stingray?" he suggested. "With two simple cuts one of those can fit into two of your square pans."

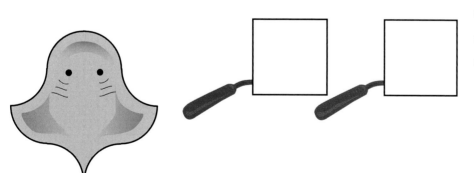

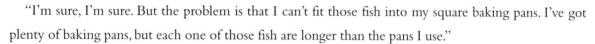

THE FISHMONGER QUICKLY WRAPPED all the fish that Ollie had chosen and handed them over. Ollie was about to move away, when he noticed that Dr. Broth was staring intently at the bundle.

"What's the matter?" asked Ollie.

Dr. Broth grabbed the fish from Ollie and let out a cry.

"Don't worry," said Dr. Brothergee. "I'm sure all the fish here are killed in a humane way."

"These are Indo-pithecine tribal-kinship equations!" shouted Dr. Broth. "This is the manuscript!"

The others leaned in to look at the fish. Sure enough, it was wrapped in a sheet of dense academic prose. Frozen with both hope and dread, they watched as Dr. Broth fondled the paper, running his finger over the letters.

But then he let out a gasp. Pointing in wordless frustration, he drew their attention to other customers leaving the fish stand. They, too, carried bundles wrapped with heavily typed 8½-by-11-inch paper. Dr. Broth made as if to chase after them. But when he looked into the immense market, he saw that there were white bundles scattered throughout the crowd.

He turned to the fishmonger.

"Where did you get this?" he demanded, pointing to the wrapper.

"I'm very sorry, sir," said the vendor, "I ran out of fish wrap, so I bought that from my cousin who's selling copies down by the courthouse."

Dr. Broth was fuming.

"Perhaps we should proceed there," suggested Dr. Brothergee.

Weaving through the crowd, Dr. Brothergee led them out of the marketplace and down a few blocks to the courthouse. On the corner a man was clearing stacks of paper off a card table and shoving them into a duffel bag.

Dr. Broth ran up to the table, furiously waving the wrapped fish.

"Is it true you're selling copies of this manuscript?" asked Dr. Broth fiercely.

"Fresh out," answered the man.

"But what are you doing with it?"

"Just making a little money, sir. People are going crazy over it. This bootleg is selling better than the screenplay of *Handicrafts of Rajasthan*."

Dr. Broth Sees His Name in Lights

"You have screenplays of *Handicrafts of Rajasthan?*" asked Dr. Brothergee.

"Here's my last copy," said the man, pulling one out of his bag. "Five rupees."

The gleeful Dr. Brothergee handed over the money and started walking home. Ollie and McGuffin trailed behind him, trying to look over his shoulder at the screenplay.

"This really is a wonderful work," said Dr. Brothergee. "Let me read you a few passages."

And so they continued down the street, Dr. Brothergee reciting lines from *Handicrafts of Rajasthan* to the receptive pair.

"Hey!" shouted Dr. Broth, "what about my manuscript!?"

Just then, a tall, beautiful, long-lashed woman in a sari tapped Dr. Broth on the shoulder.

"Excuse me," she said nervously, "are you . . . are you he? You are! Oh! Could I have your autograph?"

Dr. Broth dazedly scrawled his name on her fish wrap.

"Oh, thank you!" exclaimed the woman, and, landing a big wet kiss on Dr. Broth's forehead, she ran off.

The stunned doctor stumbled after her. "How do you know who I am?" he shouted.

"Everybody knows who you are," she said, pointing across the street.

A movie house with a giant marquee loomed at them. The words *Dr. Broth's Indo-pithecine Tribal-kinship Equations* glowed from above. Posters with Dr. Broth's face hung on the walls of the theater. A few cars passed by with Dr. Broth bumper stickers; a billboard in the distance advertised Dr. Broth's Non-Euclidean Paleolinguistic Astrohistoriographic Theme Park.

A crowd was forming around the doctor. Some of them wore Broth baseball caps, others had on T-shirts emblazoned with the equations themselves. The crowd grew and grew as Dr. Broth fans came running from all directions. He was soon swept away on their shoulders.

DR. BROTHERGEE, OLLIE, MCGUFFIN and Dr. Broth stood outside Dr. Brothergee's house. A black limousine pulled up to take Dr. Broth to an exclusive TV interview.

"Are you sure you don't want to come back to New York with us?" asked Ollie as Dr. Broth climbed into the absurdly long car.

"I don't think there's much chance of me getting this kind of reception there," said the doctor. "Thank

On to Higher Things

you, but I'm going to stay for an extended sabbatical. Keep the garden nice and Euclidean, Ollie."

Dr. Broth's limo sped away, filling the air with dust.

"I guess we *should* tend to the topiary," said Ollie as they retired to Dr. Brothergee's veranda for one last Mango lassie before the journey home.

10 ACHOCOLATE NOW!

The first chocolate can be divided quite easily—into four equilateral triangles, each of which contains two nuts. The second chocolate is more complicated.

11 DIE BETTING

The first four rolls (and their scores) were:

Venus-Earth, Mars-Venus, Moon-Moon—one
Sun-Mars, Venus-Venus, Earth-Venus—two
Moon-Moon, Earth-Moon, Sun-Mars—one
Earth-Earth, Moon-Mars, Venus-Venus—zero

If the Venus-Venus pair is invalid, the Sun-Mars and Earth-Venus pairs both score points. That's why the crowd heckled the urchin: He blew a chance to score two by pairing up his Earths and his Venuses. When Dr. Broth rolled, Ollie saw that he had one winning pair (Sun-Mars) and deduced that the Moons and the Mercuries would pair up for two more winning pairs.

14 RIFF TIFF

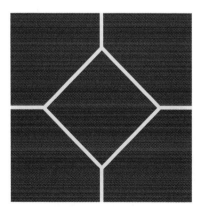

15 REST IN PEACE

The message is hidden in the notes of the music. The sixteenth notes take on the letter value of the notes on the staff from top to bottom. **E, F, G, A, B, C, D, E, F.** The eighth notes represent the letters **L, M, N, H, I, J, K, L,** and **M** (on the same lines and spaces). The quarter notes on the staff represent the letters **S, T, U, O, P, Q, R, S,** and **T**, and the half notes equal **Z** on the first line, **V** on the second space, **W** on the third line, **X** on the third space, **Y** on the fourth line and **Z** on the fourth space. The quarter-note rests and half-note rests represent commas and periods, respectively. The notes in the song can be decoded to read: "Alpaca steaks, alpaca stew./Eat it once, and nothing else will do./Beat its friends, if they put up a fight./Let's eat, alpaca, tonight."

17 SINGEING IN THE RAIN

Given that McGuffin and the urchins are the quickest and Dr. Broth is the slowest, the sequence that allows for the speediest trip without leaving Ollie, Broth, or McGuffin in danger of attack is:

First side	in route	the other side
OMB	UU◊	
OMB	◊U	U
UBO	M◊	U
UBO	◊U	M
UB	UO◊	M
UB	◊O	UM
U	OB◊	UM
U	◊U	OMB
	UU◊	OMB

O=Ollie; M=McGuffin; B=Dr. Broth; U=Urchin

20 NO LEFTIES IN MOSCOW

22 BATHROOM BUREAUCRACY

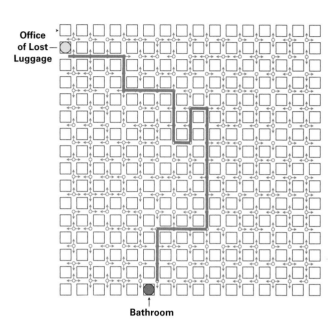

24 A BLUEPRINT FOR DISASTER

Five out of six blueprints are of the same building. However, the fourth-floor plan has the southeast tower in the northeast corner, and must belong to a separate plan.

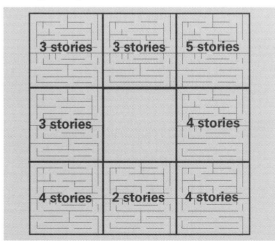

27 NUMBER ONE OR NUMBER TWO?

29 STRANDED

The strands overlap to make the sequence: **GTA ACA TTC CGA TCA**.

31 HUMOROUS DNA

The strands for the humerus overlap to make the sequence: **TCA GCA TTC AAG AAG TAC GTA CTG TTC TTC**.

32 HUMAN OR ALPACA?

The sequence is human, not alpaca.

33 CLONESOMES

One district needs to have fourteen Conservatives and fourteen Labourites. The other three have nine Conservatives, nine Labourites, and ten Haggis Nationalists. One way to redraw the districts is shown here:

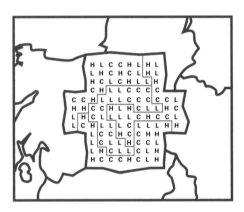

36 MAMA AN' THE PAPAS

A comparison of the DNA from the mother and the child show two short sections of disagreement. These genes must have come from the father. Only Bulbous Nose's DNA has the correct base pairs in that position. He must be the father.

41 FOR WHOM THE TOLLS BILL

There are no tolls if the route passes through intersections **A, H, V, U, T, N, O, R, S** (19.5 km). The shortest route goes through intersections **A, D, G, H, I, J, O, R, S** (9.5 km). The cheapest route (with petrol costing 50p/litre and the car getting 10 km/litre) goes through intersections **A, H, V, R, S** (12.5 km and 25p). The fastest route (at 60 km per hour and a two-minute delay at each tollbooth) goes through intersections **D, G, H, I, N, O, R**, and **S** (10 km plus one tollbooth for 12 minutes total).

43 CRASH PAD

There are three combinations that destroy the robots: circle to white, black to black, and square to circle. There is only one path to the rocket that does not contain this combination.

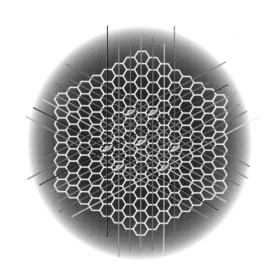

45 JUMPING AHEAD

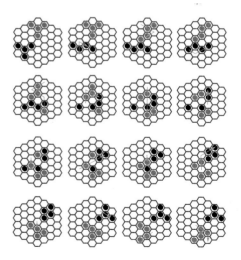

48 A MERCURIAL ETHERFORCE

49 TOUCHING BASE ON MERCURY

a) 4 + 4 = 10 in base eight

or b) 4 x 4 = 10 in base sixteen

c) 6 + 2 = 10 in base eight

or d) 6 x 2 = 10 in base twelve

e) 8 + 2 = 10 in base ten

or f) 8 x 2 = 10 in base sixteen

But because 8 + 12 + 10 = 30 in base ten, the correct equations are a, d, and e.

52 INTRODUCTORY REMARKS

If you take the first letter from each word in Dr. Broth's speech, you get the message: "These lights are hot. My throat is dry. I need some water."

53 QUESTIONABLE ANSWER SESSION

A	L	P	H	A		O	M	E	G	A
L	I	L	A	C		M	U	L	E	S
P	L	U	T	O		E	L	E	C	T
H	A	T	E	R		G	E	C	K	O
A	C	O	R	N		A	S	T	O	R

55 THREE FEET WIDE AND RISING

Raising the track three inches off the surface of the planet means adding six inches to the diameter of the track (that is, three inches plus the diameter of the planet plus three inches). The length of the track is merely the diameter times π, so about nineteen inches of additional track will be needed.

56 ROLLING RATS

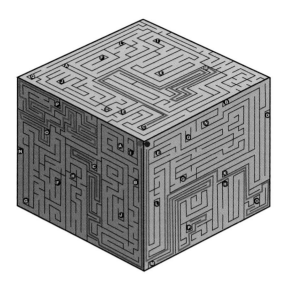

57 RETURN TO SENDER

The signs overlap to form *NY*.

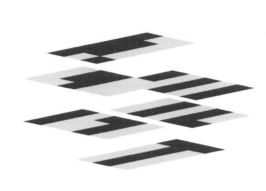

59 SEVENTY MILLION MILES TO HOME

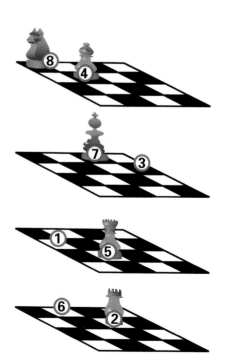

61 FAST-FOLD RESTAURANT

Fold the note as shown below. Read each letter in order to spell out the message. The note says, "KNOW WHEN TO FOLD 'EM."

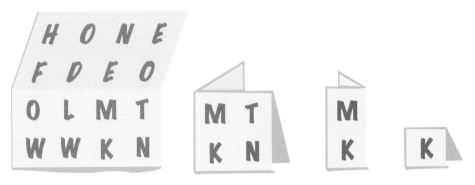

62 A VOLUME DISCOUNT

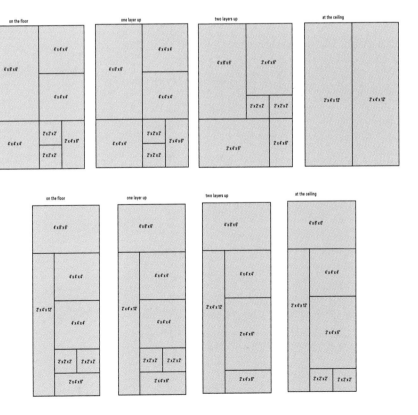

64 WINDOW OF THE SOUL

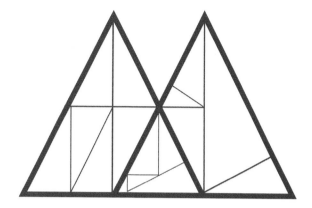

66 RESTORING ORDER

Givens:

Batting and position: (a) P hits 9th. (b) LF, CF, RF hit 1st through 6th. (c) SS hits 2nd. (d) RF hits 1st through 3rd. (e) 2B hits 6th. (f) 1B hits 4th. Batting and players: (g) Gomez hits 1st through 3rd. (h) Heap hits before Douglas, who hits before Iverson (i) Fitzgerald before Heap (j) Earl before Archer (k) Iverson hits 7th. Players and position: (l) Benitez plays CF. (m) Archer plays 2B. (n) Cooper either C or 1B (o) Double plays usually go Gomez to Archer to Douglas.

Deductions:

(p) Outfielders hit 1st, 3rd, and 5th (from b, c, e, and f). (q) Archer hits 6th (from e and m). (r) Earl hits 5th (from j). (s) Because Gomez is usually involved with double plays (from o), he is probably not an outfielder.

Conclusions:

(t) Gomez is SS and hits 2nd (from c, g, and p). (u) Because most double plays involve the first baseman, Douglas is 1B and hits 4th (from o and f). (v) Heap hits first (from h and i). (w) Fitzgerald hits 9th (from v). (x) Benitez hits 3rd (from l, p, r, and u). (y) Cooper hits 8th.

Lineup:

1.	Heap	RF	6.	Archer	2B
2.	Gomez	SS	7.	Iverson	3B
3.	Benitez	CF	8.	Cooper	C
4.	Douglas	1B	9.	Fitzgerald	P
5.	Earl	LF			

68 THE COPPER CON

71 A BRONX TAIL

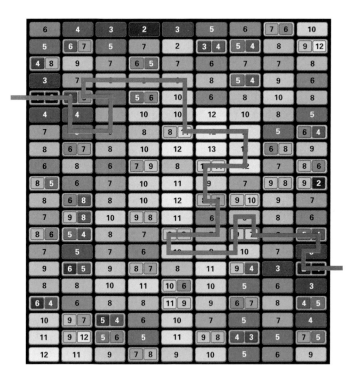

74 BACKWARD KNIGHTS AND KNAVES

The nonpalindrome number is 196.

77 RISE ILL? O.K. OLLIE, SIR.

"Oh, cameras are macho."

78 A DADA

"Name not, stoneman."

82 A TROUBLED BRIDGE OVER WATER

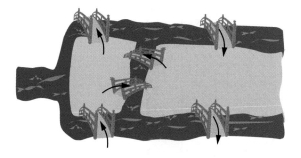

79 PIECE OF CAKE

Eight identical pieces can be cut as shown:

84 BRAWNY BRIDGE

The problem with Dr. Broth's proposal is that while the strength of a building material increases in proportion to its cross-section, its weight increases in proportion to its volume. A bridge that is three times larger in every direction is only one-third as strong.

84 A HEX LESSON

A slice through the midpoints of six of the eight edges of a cube will make two two-dimensional hexagonal faces.

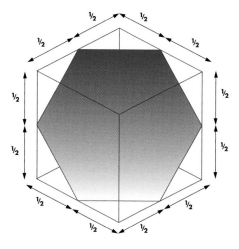

86 CORNERED

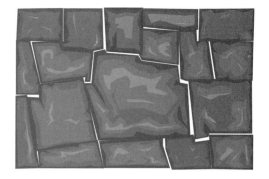

89 A BELT OF GENIUS

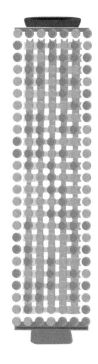

91 A BEND IN THE RIVER

93 CON CAVE SEARCH

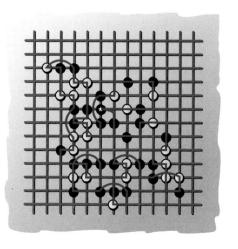

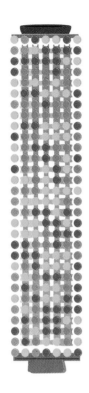

94 BELTED AGAIN

97 THE PRIEST OF FORETHOUGHT

THE IDIOTS' CRUISE

100 WRANGLE IN TIME

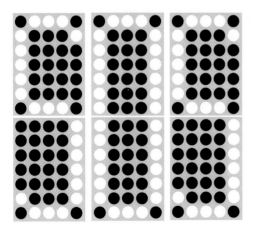

102 WHAT MORTALS THESE FOOLS BE

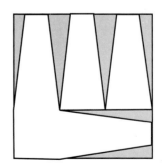

105 KETTLE POWER

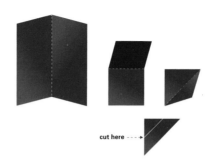

cut here - - - - ►

106 I WANT SOME SEAFOOD, MAMA

108 URCHIN AVERSION

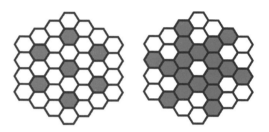

REVOLUTIONARY FRANCE

110 SOME GAULLE

Across:

1. Carp + Begat; 6. A + P + Hid; 9. D(EP)OT; 10. NASA Trout (anagram) = Sally Ride; 11. Singin' (anagram) + N; 12. Car Tore (anagram); 13. O + Pie; 15. Change or a (anagram); 18. Yes new ark (anagram); 20. In + dy; 22. A (guess - U) + 1e; 24. GRE + (Merlin - ER); 26. Oboes + in + S.S. (anagram); 27. sev(en nui)sances; 28. Ray + on; 29. Noticing (anagram) + O;

Down

1. CD idea (anagram); 2. Rip + E + N (east and north); 3. E + teen (anagram) + NT; 4. Began - g + s + talk; 5. Gat + or; 6. H(avoc ado)nis; 7. Hand + (earth - h) + 1; 8. Ted (reversal) + erred; 14. P + Serbs say (anagram); 16. C + Nice orgy (anagram); 17. P(a ram)our; 19. Mere (anagram) + son; 20. Ic + beer (anagram) + G; 21. In + God (anagram) + I; 23. Sci + if (reversal); 25. LA + in a (anagram)

114 CONQUER AND DIVIDE

A square can be divided into any number of equal parts. The key is to create triangles that have one vertex at the center of the square and that have bases of equal length along the perimeter. Because the area of a triangle equals half the height times the base, each triangle will have an equal area.

115 CAPTIVITY, INEQUALITY, MISANTHROPY

Playground

Both
Segments
Equal

116 HEAD CHOPPERS AND CODE BREAKERS

The solution is based on a simple binary code (00001 = A, 00010 = B, 00011 = C, 00100 = D, 00101 = E, etc.). The code numbers are then placed into ten rows of five numbers each. The digits of numbers directly above are added to the digits of the numbers below like so: 10011 + 00110 = 10121. The result are trinary numbers arrayed in a five-by-nine grid. The message can be decoded to read: Release the captives if you want to see your teddy bear again.

R	E	L	E	A
10010	00101	01100	00101	00001
20021	00202	11200	01101	00102
S	E	T	H	E
10011	00101	10100	01000	00101
10022	00102	20100	11100	01102
C	A	P	T	I
00011	00001	10000	10100	01001
10121	00102	20011	11101	01111
V	E	S	I	F
10110	00101	10011	01001	00110
21111	01212	20112	11112	00111
Y	O	U	W	A
11001	01111	10101	10111	00001
12111	11211	20201	11222	10012
N	T	T	O	S
01110	10100	10100	01111	10011
01211	10201	21101	02222	20112
E	E	Y	O	U
00101	00101	11001	01111	10101
10111	10201	11102	01211	10201
R	T	E	D	D
10010	10100	00101	00100	00100
21011	10110	00202	00101	10110
Y	B	E	A	R
11001	00010	00101	00001	10010
11002	00121	00102	01002	11120
A	G	A	I	N
00001	00111	00001	01001	01110

118 A MESMERIZING PERFORMANCE

A close approximation of a spiral can be made by stacking layers of four tiles—two black, two white—offsetting each layer by 45 degrees. The result looks like this:

121 A WILD SUGGESTION

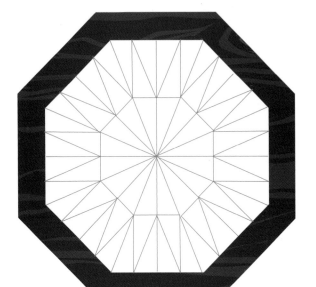

PLANET OF THE ALPACAS

123 AN UNEXPECTED TURN

Turn the tray ninety degrees to the left. In the spaces between the dents, the ape has spelled

C	O	U	N
T	E	R	C
L	O	C	K
W	I	S	E

or *counterclockwise*.

126 CELL WALLS

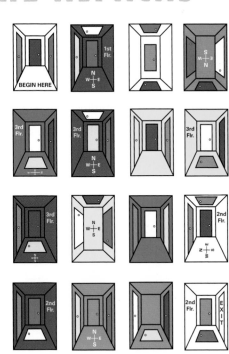

128 SPITMUS TEST

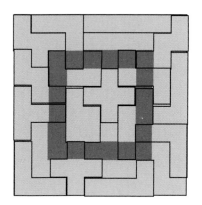

132 SPLATTERED

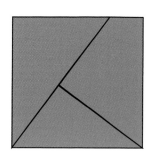 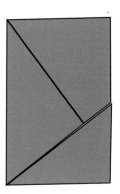

134 THE HOSPITTLE

To reduce the average waiting time, the appointments should be scheduled so that the quickest go first and the longest go last:

Name	Appointment Length	Waiting Time
Williams	15 min.	0 min.
Quartey	20 min.	15 min.
Smith	30 min.	35 min.
Gupta	40 min.	65 min.
Jones	45 min.	105 min.
Kwan	60 min.	150 min.

Average Waiting Time: 61 min., 40 sec.

136 GYPSY GEOGRAPHY

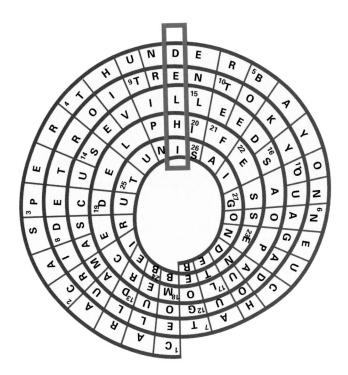

138 LOST IN SPACE-TIME

The key is to have the younger twin arrive two years ahead of the older twin. Because people traveling at the speed of light do not experience the passage of time, the older twin will remain just shy of his thirty-eighth birthday until he arrives, while the twin who arrived first will age from thirty-six to thirty-eight. Here's the path each twin should take:

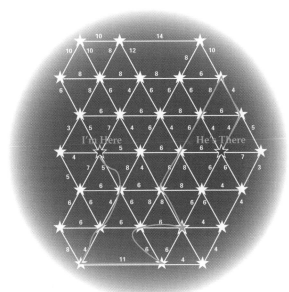

140 ONCE UPON A PRIME IN ITALY

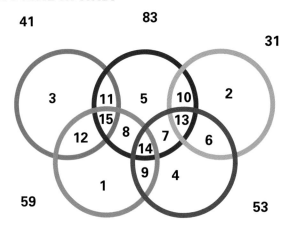

41   83   31

3   11   5   10   2

15   13

12   8   7   6

14

9   4

1

59   53

41+83+31+59+53=267

143 THE PRINCIPLES OF SEATING

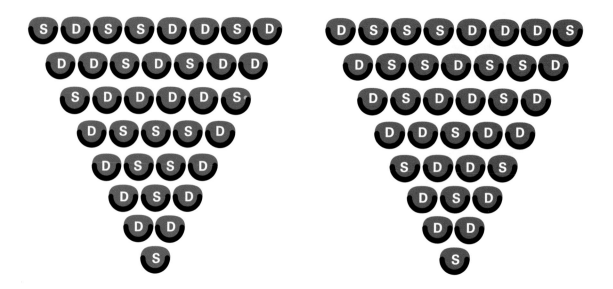

144 ORDERING OFF THE MENU

This is one way to get seventeen sections from the intersection of the three triangles:

145 NUMBERS SPEAK

The letters correspond to these numbers:

A = 2, E = 3, B = 5, L = 7, N = 11, S = 13,
J = 17, V = 43, D = 197, R = 403

147 PRIME GEARS

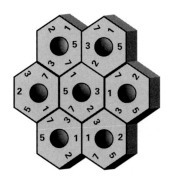

150 TAKES A LICKING, KEEPS ON CASTING A SHADOW

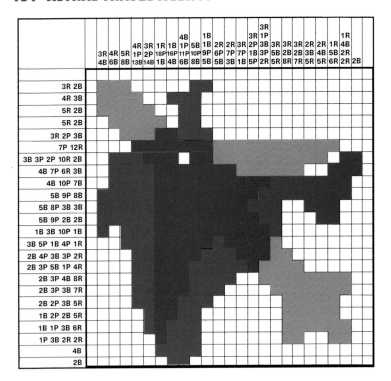

| | | 3R 4B | 4R 6B | 5R 8B | 4R 1P 13B | 3R 2P 14B | 1R 18P 1B | 1B 16P 4B | 4B 1P 11P 6B | 5B 10P 8B | 1B 1B 9P 5B | 2R 6P 3B | 2R 7P 1B | 3R 7P 5P | 3R 1P 3B 2R | 5B 5R | 3R 2B 8R | 3R 2B 7R | 2R 5R | 2R 5R | 1R 4B 6R | 1R 4B 2R | 2B |

3R 2B
4R 3B
5R 2B
5R 2B
3R 2P 3B
7P 12R
3B 3P 2P 10R 2B
4B 7P 6R 3B
4B 10P 7B
5B 9P 8B
5B 8P 3B 3B
5B 9P 2B 2B
1B 3B 10P 1B
3B 5P 1B 4P 1R
2B 4P 3B 3P 2R
2B 3P 5B 1P 4R
2B 3P 4B 8R
2B 3P 3B 7R
2B 2P 3B 5R
1B 2P 2B 5R
1B 1P 3B 6R
1P 3B 2R 2R
4B
2B

INDIA, NOW

The circles spell: Circumstance,

Continuation, Satisfaction

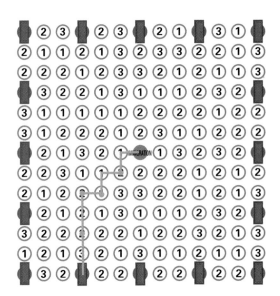